"TERROR STRUCK

when I saw her standing above me, only a few feet away from the edge of the rocks. If she were startled, she might step back and. . . .

"Her eyes were wild. I tried to pull her away, and as I did she caught my shoulder and pulled me upward toward the edge of the cliff. I tried to wrench myself away from her, but her fingers were like iron nails driven into my body. Her strength was the strength of madness.

"The cold chill of death overcame me. The edge of the cliff could not be far behind her now. In a moment, in seconds, both of us would tumble over the edge. . . ."

Other SIGNET Gothics by Mary Linn Roby

The
Broken Key

by

Mary Linn Roby

A SIGNET BOOK
NEW AMERICAN LIBRARY
TIMES MIRROR

Library of Congress Catalog Card Number: 72-7770.

Published by arrangement with the author.

 SIGNET TRADEMARK REG. U.S. PAT. OFF. AND FOREIGN COUNTRIES
REGISTERED TRADEMARK—MARCA REGISTRADA
HECHO EN CHICAGO, U.S.A.

SIGNET, SIGNET CLASSICS, SIGNETTE, MENTOR AND PLUME BOOKS
are published by The New American Library, Inc.,
1301 Avenue of the Americas, New York, New York 10019

FIRST PRINTING, MAY, 1974

1 2 3 4 5 6 7 8 9

PRINTED IN THE UNITED STATES OF AMERICA

The
Broken Key

CHAPTER

1

It was twilight when I first saw Pennarth, and a storm was blowing in off the Atlantic. I had been driving for hours through inland lanes, hedged with hawthorn and overhung by the thick, rain-drenched leaves of massive oaks. Only when I finally emerged onto the coast road did I comprehend the stark wilderness of Cornwall.

To the right of the car the land plunged off in a rocky mass into the foaming sea. To my left the country lay flat and bare except for a few wind-stunted trees that bent unresistingly as the gale buffeted them. And high on a jutting promontory stood the house, blank-eyed in the gathering dusk, its turreted rooftop caught in the swirling mist.

I braked the car by the iron barrier of a gate, its spiked bars glittering with moisture in the glow of my headlights. On each side of the gate itself a high stone wall stretched into the shadows, huge blocks of granite encrusted with moss and overhung with a wilderness of bushes.

I pushed at the gate, and it swung back slowly on rust-ing hinges, its base scraping against the rough gravel of the weed-lined drive, now little more than a path that led up to the house. There was an atmosphere of desertion about the place that I had not expected, despite the fact that the solicitor had described the estate to me in detail when I had gone to see him in London two weeks before.

"There are extensive grounds," he had said, "and as I understand it, the cottage is quite a distance from the main house. It's not the original gatehouse. From what Miss Randolph told me I take it that that building has been allowed to fall into ruins. Your legacy, Miss Grey, housed the gardener and his family when Pennarth was fully staffed. It's quite isolated. As a younger woman Miss Ran-dolph went there occasionally despite her—er—falling out with her family. I remember her telling me that she was never disturbed, and it should be the same as far as you're concerned. The old man is a recluse now, at any rate, from what I hear. Of course, I'll write and tell them you intend to take residence in the cottage, but there shouldn't be any need for you to visit Pennarth—the actual house itself—unless you want to."

I had known that he was trying to tell me that it might be awkward if I did, that it was doubtful whether Miss Randolph's brother would be pleased to have a stranger living anywhere on the grounds of his estate, especially if that stranger had been a friend of a sister to whom he had not spoken in over fifty years.

"I want you to have the cottage as a studio, my dear," Miss Randolph had told me, her pinched face gray against the pillows of the hospital bed. "You've been more than simply a paid companion to me, you know. And I realize how difficult it's been for you, trying to scrape out a living here in London and still have time for your painting. You need a place of your own where you can be quiet and work. You're young now, but the years pass so quickly. The little that your father left you would be enough, wouldn't it, if you had the cottage as a studio?"

I had not tried to dissuade her from leaving it to me. My parents died while I was attending the Slade in London. The frequent visits initiated by their illnesses and subsequent deaths to the little house in the Somerset village where my father had been a physician for his entire life had resurrected so many aching memories that I was relieved by the sale of the house and the knowledge that I would never return to the village again. I had been glad of the need to work hard at any job I could get—commercial artwork for the most part. But gradually I had come to yearn for the time to paint, and this was what Miss Randolph was offering me: time and a place that was beautiful. During the three years I had cared for the old woman, she had told me much about Cornwall. She had been young there, and her descriptions captured the wild beauty of the rocky coastline and the sea. She had not talked much about Pennarth itself, because her later memories were unhappy ones. There had been legal disputes when her father had died many years before, and she had been left with only a small legacy and the cottage that she intended to will to me.

"My mother, poor soul, insisted on leaving some of her furniture to me," she had told me, her thin hands pinching the sheets. "These pieces are still there. You won't have to buy anything, and there's a north window in the attic on the second floor. You should be able to paint there the way you've always wanted to. Don't refuse to take this from me, Sara. It's all I can give you, and you've given me so much."

Three days later she died of a second stroke. I had promised her that I would have her few belongings at the flat on Wigmore Street taken care of—the books crated and sent to a nursing home and the furniture given to the Salvation Army. There were no personal papers. On the day before she was taken to the hospital, I helped her burn them. Once, I believed, the velvet jewelry box in her bedroom contained some rings and broaches she inherited from her mother, but nothing was left.

Although she never told me so, I think she found it difficult to stretch the little capital she possessed to cover the necessities of life during the past few years, and perhaps the jewelry had been sold. All the time I worked in the little flat, packing and cleaning, I kept imagining that I heard the echo of her laughter, for although she was very weak during the last years of her life, she had never lost her childlike gaiety. I found that I missed her even more than I imagined that I would.

The remainder of the winter was a wretched time, colored with the grayness of the fog that coated the city and pressed its hands against the windows of my bed-sitter in Earl's Court. I spent the days attempting to paint and seeing a few friends, all of whom, during those months, seemed to be as infected with the general gloom as I.

I had saved enough to make it possible for me not to take another job at once, but I knew that if I should not come into possession of the cottage, I would have to find something to do, and that I would probably never have the time to paint as I had always hoped to do. The money my father had left me was not enough to sustain me, even in the country, if I had to pay rent. Miss Randolph had talked about the cottage, true, but I could not be certain she had taken any steps toward making it mine. Or there might be legal complications, since the building was actually on the Pennarth estate. By March I had disbanded my hopes and determined to find a job.

Then the letter from Miss Randolph's solicitor arrived. The next day I walked out of his rooms in the Inns of Court and across a quadrangle bright with daffodils, my mind focused on the future for the first time in years.

Suddenly everything seemed to come right. I wrote to the only people I knew in Cornwall, a girl with whom I had been friends in art school who was now married to Greg, a young sculptor. Bertha had written back, telling me I would never regret leaving London, and she urged me to visit them as soon as I was settled.

As a postscript Bertha added that Greg's father was giving Greg a car as a birthday present, an old runabout but something that would serve as transportation. His father could not deliver it to them himself, and there was no one else in the family available for the task. If I was willing, I could drive down in it when I came to take possession of the cottage.

"It would be far the simplest way for you to make the move," Bertha had written in her sprawling hand, "and you would be doing us a favor, as well."

So I had driven, singing, through the suburbs of London this April morning, leaving the city behind without a backward look. I lunched on sandwiches on a hill with a view of Salisbury Cathedral before me, its spire piercing the sky beyond the water meadows. I was so happy I scarcely noticed the gathering clouds as I steered the aging vehicle along the twisting roads that crossed the barren moors beyond Chagford. Although I was exhausted, I was still singing as I drove under a gray sky through the lush hedgerows of Devon, passing one white-cottaged village after another like milestones.

I had not tried to visualize what I would find at Pennarth. I realized that the house was an ancient one, the original structure having been built in the sixteenth century, with various unmatched wings added by each successive generation. Miss Randolph had told me that. And I had imagined—I am not certain what—but it was certainly not this fog-shrouded block of stones that loomed above me malevolently, fanned by windswept trees. Suddenly all the eagerness I felt was gone, and I was aware only of an inexpressible weariness and a vague apprehension.

I was aware that I could turn the car around and go to St. Ives to spend the night with Bertha and Greg. The understanding had been that I would keep the car as long as I needed it to get settled, but I knew they would welcome me even without advance notice. Bertha would feed

me and mother me as she had done when she and Greg
were still living in London, and in the morning I could
come back and see the place as it really was and not as
some grotesquery from a half-forgotten nightmare.

But I did not want to do that. I had come so far,
determined to be settled by nightfall in the first home I
had had since I was a child. I would be a fool to let the
house above me frighten me away. Pennarth and the people in it meant nothing to me. The fog was only fog, the
wind only wind. And the crashing sound—I could hear it
now that I was outside the car. How had I expected the
sea to sound in a storm?

Somehow, I was reluctant to drive the car through the
rusting gate. Perhaps I would not make the proper turns
and find myself before the porte cochere of Pennarth.
Better first to explore on foot. According to the directions
that the solicitor had given me, the cottage should be on a
path that led to the right beyond the ruins of the gatehouse.

"Not more than five hundred feet," he had told me,
"according to the directions Miss Randolph drew up. She
sketched a plan of the grounds of the estate for me, which,
of course, you may have. The point is, you'll be near the
road. There'll be no question of your comings and goings
disturbing old Mr. Randolph. I made that point quite clear
in my letter to him."

I had assumed then that there must have been objec-
tions on the part of the family to the terms of the will.
Miss Randolph had told me that her brother's son and his
wife lived with him, and I had guessed there was enmity
between her and them as well. But I had asked no questions, and the solicitor had offered no information. Although he displayed a patina of old-world politeness, he
had made no secret of the fact that he was a busy man.

None of that mattered now, however. There was no
need to take the sketch of the estate out of my pocket-
book. I had pored over the strip of paper often enough,

tracing with my eyes the shaky lines Miss Randolph had drawn to designate a clump of trees here, a wall there, this gate, the gravel path beyond, the house above me. I knew there was supposed to be the ruin of a gatehouse beyond the gate to my right, but it was only when I was close to it that I saw the shadowy outlines of what had once been a large stone building. Now vines seemed to strangle what remained, and long grass protruded from the gaps that had once been the windows of the lower floor.

I wondered if the cottage had been kept in decent repair. Miss Randolph had told me that a man from the village who had been an undergardener at the estate agreed to go over the place yearly and make all necessary repairs. He had, at any rate, accepted her yearly check, for I had mailed the last three she had sent him. Now, however, I realized that I should be prepared to find something quite different from the tidy house I had imagined.

But it was just as she had described it. At the end of the path stretching behind the ruins of the gatehouse I came quite suddenly upon it—a tiny cottage, half hidden by the mist, hedged by neatly clipped cedars. A thickly thatched roof overhung the latticed windows. Even veiled by fog, there was something comfortingly familiar about it.

It had begun to rain in earnest now. The wind pushed against me as I made my way to the low-posted door, and I groped in the pocket of my jacket for the key. But I was no longer afraid. As I twisted the knob in my hand and the door swung open, I smelled the fragrance of old wood and lavender and knew I had come home.

There was dust everywhere, but within a second it was forgotten as I gazed around the little sitting room into which the front door opened directly. The cottage ceiling was low and black-beamed, and the walls were white stucco. Tiny windows were set deep into the wall, and their panes were closely mullioned, forming a rich pattern of crisscrossed lead. The drapes were of a thick rough red material that had been darkened to scarlet by time, and below each window a cushioned bench, set close against the wall, was covered with the same cloth.

Two deep easy chairs covered in faded-yellow monk's cloth faced one another on each side of an inglenooked fireplace of fieldstone. A round table was in the center of the room, laid with a dusty blue cloth as though whoever had eaten there last had lingered only long enough to put away the plates. There was no other furniture except an oak bookcase, too large for the room, filled with old books, their gilt titles faded into obscurity. That and a tiny end table beside one of the easy chairs completed the decor. I felt an almost unbearable flood of happiness.

The kitchen was to my left, an uncluttered little room with a low iron sink, a tiny gas range, and an ancient refrigerator that wheezed into life when I plugged the cord into the wall socket. There were two windows here, both draped with the same faded-red cloth I had seen in the sitting room, and beside one of them was a tiny oilcloth-covered table and a single wicker chair. The only large piece of furniture in the room was a huge oak sideboard of the sort often found in farm kitchens. Blue patterned plates were lined neatly along its top, and over them, hanging from hooks screwed into the wall, were cups. A quick glance in the cupboards below the sink revealed a sufficiency of pots and pans. I was suddenly aware of a pang of hunger and remembered the few foodstuffs in the trunk of the car.

I knew I should go back and move the car from its awkward stance in front of the gate, but the gravel road leading to the main house did not look as if it were frequently used, and I felt I could not leave the cottage without first seeing the upper floor. The staircase with its shallow worn steps was so narrow that my arms, even held at my side, nearly touched the wall on both sides.

At the top I groped for a wall switch and found one. A single lamp came alive at the far end of the long attic room, and I stared with pleasure at the broad-boarded floor, covered here and there with thick shaggy blue rugs, and at the old-fashioned iron-framed bedstead, the mattress of which sank invitingly in the center beneath a gaily colored patchwork quilt. There were two tiny windows on each side of the long room, mullioned like those below, but at the farther end a broad window filled the end of the attic.

During the day, I realized, this window must provide the north light Miss Randolph had mentioned. And she was right. If I were to move the bed to this end of the room and set up my easel next to the window, I would have an ideal studio.

I hated to leave the cottage, even for a few minutes, but I had to move the car and bring at least a few of my things into the house. Perhaps it was the thick walls or the thatch roof, but the sounds of the storm were muted in here. Once I opened the door, however, the full force of the gale struck me, and the sound of the surf thudded like drumbeats against my ears.

It was nearly dark now, and I could not see the sky. I ran down the path with the fog thick against my face, hoping I would not lose my way. Suddenly I saw the ruins of the gatehouse and the glow of the headlights I had forgotten to turn off. Wrenching the door open, I slid into the driver's seat, thinking that I would not try to maneuver the car inside the half-open gate but rather leave it on the verge of the road. I had started the motor before I realized there was someone in the seat beside me.

I think I must have cried out, and when I did, a woman laughed. I could just make out the outline of her dark hair and the pale oval of her face. A hand slipped over mine as it rested on the wheel. Long smooth fingers touched my arm lightly.

"Don't be afraid," she said. "The fog was so thick, and the wind always frightens me. I thought perhaps if I rested for a while it would clear a bit."

Her voice was low and evenly modulated, yet I sensed a sort of stress behind it as though she were trying too hard to maintain an effect. Even now that my eyes were adjusting to the dusk, I could not see her face clearly, but I could smell the expensive odor of her scent.

"Are you from the village?" I asked, aware of an intense desire to get her out of the car any way that I could, even if it meant driving her back there. I had drawn my hand away from under hers, but there was something about her presence that seemed to envelop me in an icy chill. As I spoke, the wind threw great drops of rain against the windshield. There was now no question of my simply ordering her out of the car.

"I'm from Pennarth," she said. "The house there on the hill. My name is Miranda Randolph."

Automatically I glanced upward at the house on the hill and saw a light spring into being behind one of the long windows, casting an eerie glow through the fog, and I realized that she must be the wife of Miss Randolph's nephew. I am not certain the old woman had ever met her, but she had mentioned her name once and as she had done so, sighed.

"Perhaps you won't mind my asking who you are," Miranda said. "I saw you coming out through the gate. Did you walk all the way up to the house? We don't often have visitors, you know. I'm so glad I got into your car. Otherwise, you see, I might have missed you."

"I'm Sara Grey," I said. "Your aunt——"

"Oh, I know who you are," the woman beside me crowed delightedly. "You're the person who's going to live at March Cottage. Paul's father was simply furious when he heard about it. He said his sister had done it just to remind him that that part of the estate doesn't belong to him. I think he expected her to leave it to him. He's such an old fool. Paul says I shouldn't say it, but it's true. I wouldn't be surprised if he isn't senile. After all, he's eighty. How was he when you talked to him? I can't bear to think of what he must have said." She laughed again, a high tinkling laugh like a child's.

"I didn't meet him or anyone," I told her. "I just arrived a few minutes ago. I went to look at the cottage."

"Oh, that was very wise of you." She twisted herself in the seat, and in the light from the dashboard I could see a long finely structured face and dark eyes that glittered under thick lashes. "Now that you've seen the cottage, will you stay?" she added in a rush. "I do hope that you will. I'm often lonely here. Paul used to promise that he'd take me to London once a month, but he doesn't even bother to promise now. Not that it matters. He never does what he tells me he'll do. I think he likes to confuse me."

The words could have been spoken bitterly, but they were not. She sounded delighted that her husband broke his promises, as if the whole thing were a great joke. I stared at her, bewildered.

"Well," Miranda Randolph said with sudden impatience, "aren't you going to invite me to the cottage? We can't very well sit here all night, can we?"

Her sudden change of mood disconcerted me absolutely, and I began pulling suitcases and clothing bags from the back seat. I did not want her in the cottage, but if she was determined to go there with me, there seemed to be no alternative. I had no intention of driving up to the front of Pennarth and depositing her there if it meant the risk of an encounter with either her husband or her father-in-law.

"All right," I said, "but if you want to come with me, you'll have to carry these. Then wait while I park the car on the verge. I don't want to block the gate."

"It's all right," she said, opening the door, cases piled against her. "I mean, no one ever comes here except the delivery van on Thursday, and that comes to the back of the house. We order everything. My father-in-law doesn't like people crawling around, as he puts it. When he knows that you've really come. . . ."

I raced the motor and backed the car away from her before she had even shut the door. Then, switching off the motor and the lights, I got out and with the wind pouring rain down the back of my raincoat collar, kicked the trunk of the car, which was, Greg's father had told me, the only way to open it. Pulling out two boxes of groceries, I piled them on top of each other, slammed the lid of the trunk shut, and pushed my way through the half-open gate. Behind me, over the sound of the wind and the surf, I heard Miranda laugh.

I was breathless by the time we reached the cottage. The rain was coming down so hard that I was nearly blinded when I raised my head to pick out the lights I had left burning. I tried to recapture the feeling of contentment I had experienced when I opened this door before. But now Miranda was behind me, pushing me into the tiny sitting room, collapsing with my suitcases on the floor, shaking her long black hair until the water flew off it in a spray.

"Oh, it's lovely!" she gasped. "How I should like to have a little house like this. I used to come down here often, you know, and peek through the windows. I know where everything is. Once when the man from the village came to clean, I crept in after him and looked around while he was working upstairs."

"I'm sure that Miss Randolph wouldn't have minded if you came in to look around," I said, setting the groceries on a shelf in the kitchen. Something about this woman made me very impatient, as one would be impatient with an affected child. I wished she would get off the floor and stop tossing her hair around. I wished she would leave. "Surely," I said, "if you wanted to see the cottage, you could have told the man so and come inside quite openly."

"You don't understand!" She seemed to fling the words, her voice suddenly tight with fury. "When he came downstairs and found me in the kitchen, he made me leave. He said he would tell my husband if I didn't. And he told me I shouldn't come around again, making a nuisance of my-

self. I expect that's what you think now—that I'm making
a nuisance of myself."

She threw her head back and stared directly at me. For
the first time I saw her face in the full light and was
shocked. In the dimness of the car I had thought that she
was young and beautiful. She *had* been beautiful, but she
was not now, and she was not young. She stared up at me,
the cords of her long neck pulled tight. There were two
deep lines on each side of her drooping mouth, and her
eyes, which were as large and brilliant as I had thought
them, were encased in gray wrinkled pouches. As for her
hair, it was too black, too glossy. It aged her face in the
way that only dyed hair can do. While I stared at her in
horror, she laughed again, that high, trilling child's laugh,
and raised herself with a single lithe movement from the
floor.

"I'll leave presently," she said in an ordinary voice.
"You'd rather not have me here, wouldn't you? Well, I can
understand that. Did you drive all the way from London
today? I heard my father-in-law saying that you were from
London. He seemed to think it would be much better all
around if you would stay there."

"Yes," I said, slipping off my raincoat. "I did drive
down from London, and I'm rather tired. Perhaps tomorrow. . . ."

"Oh, I'll be down every day," Miranda Randolph said,
smiling. Her moods were mercurial. She was a strange
ghostlike sight, standing there just inside the door, her
light summer dress, which seemed to be nothing more nor
less than an ordinary cotton housedress, clinging, wet, to
her thin, breastless body. She was very tall, taller by half a
head than I, and somehow the fact that I had to look up to
her as I would to a man when we talked added to my
desire to have her gone. Perhaps it would be better to
make it clear right now that I intended to be busy every
day and that frequent visits on her part would not be
welcome.

Yet how do you say something like that to a woman

who is obviously lonely and unhappy? Some people could
have found the words, but I could not. Besides, there was
something about her sudden changes of mood that frightened me. It was impossible to know how she might react
to the suggestion that she leave now, and with the rain
beating on the windows it would be, at the very least,
inhospitable.

Accordingly, I made tea for both of us on the tiny gas
range and fixed bacon and scrambled eggs. Miranda,
meanwhile, disappeared with my suitcases up the stairs,
and I heard her exclaiming to herself about the coziness of
the attic bedroom. As I set the table in the sitting room, I
was aware that although she was rather odd, I was not
altogether displeased to have someone share my first meal
in this cottage. The frequency of her future visits could be
handled when the time came. Standing at the foot of the
narrow stairs, I could hear her singing something that
sounded like a ballad, a strange song that melted into the
sound of the wind. She came running down the stairs in
bare feet, and I saw that she had taken off her wet clothes
and was wearing an orange woolen dressing gown of mine
that hung ludicrously just below her knees.

"After we've eaten," she said happily, settling herself at
the table, "we'll light a fire in the fireplace, and I'll dry my
things. There's wood in the boxroom behind the kitchen.
Did you know that? I saw the man put it there last autumn."

She began to eat greedily before I had even taken my
chair opposite her. Although she must have been fifteen
years older than I, I was beginning to react toward her as
one would to an irresponsible child. It occurred to me to
wonder if she was totally sane. At the very least, she was
certainly an individualist.

"Won't your husband be worried?" I asked her. The tea
was steaming hot and strong, and that and the food made
me feel more self-assured.

She raised her head and stared at me with those

strangely glittering eyes, and her face fell suddenly into harsh lines. "You want me to leave!" she said accusingly. "Why didn't you say so before? You're like all the others."

"It's storming," I said patiently. "You went out for a walk, didn't you? How long ago?"

"Not long," she said sullenly. "After tea. I wanted scones for tea, but Mrs. Herrick never pays any attention to what I tell her. She hates me."

"When you don't come back, they'll be worried," I repeated. Suddenly I was no longer hungry. There was something more here than simple eccentricity.

Miranda finished the last of her eggs and pushed her plate away violently. Her fork clattered to the floor. "Paul will think that I lost my way in the fog," she said darkly. "Perhaps he'll think I fell off a cliff into the sea. That would make him happy. Sometimes I dream about that happening, and afterward he laughs. Not in front of the others. But when he's alone, he laughs. Sometimes when I wake up, I can hear him laughing."

"That's nonsense," I said sharply without thinking.

"You don't know anything about it," the woman said shrilly. Rising, she began to pace back and forth across the room, her dark head bent. "Perhaps I exaggerate," she went on in a more reasonable tone. "I expect you think I'm rather strange. Most people do."

Her remarks were too direct. I did not know how to deal with them, and yet to snub her seemed wrong. She might be mad. I could not be sure. If she was, it seemed unthinkable that her husband would allow her to wander about alone. All that I was really certain of was that she was being more open than people generally are with strangers, that she was making herself vulnerable, that she wanted some sort of reassurance.

"You're different," I said slowly, pouring more tea for both of us. "I've never met anyone like you before, but I don't think you are strange. It must be a lonely life here."

"Ah!" She stopped her pacing and turned on me, her

dark eyes blazing with sudden passion. "I wondered how long it would be before you'd start to ask questions. You needn't bother to try, you know. I can keep secrets. Paul thinks I can't, but I can." Her face went through one of those metamorphoses with which I was becoming familiar. She smiled slyly. "I know a good deal more than they think I know," she said. "I could tell you everything you've come here to find out if I wanted to."

"Listen to me," I said, rising. "Miss Randolph, your husband's aunt, was a close friend of mine. She left me this cottage because she knew I desperately needed a place where I could live in quiet and paint. I don't know why you think I'm here, but that's the reason. I don't want to know any secrets. And now I think you'd better let me drive you up to Pennarth."

It was as if I had struck her. She seemed to droop, her arms hanging limp at her sides, her head bowed. When we heard knocking at the door, she did not move. My heart suddenly pounding hard, I went to open it. A man stood on the doorstep, the mist glistening on his dark hair. The collar of his raincoat was turned high about his face, but I could see the strong even features and the grim line of his mouth.

"I'm Paul Randolph," he said, looking past me. "I see that my wife is here." He stepped past me into the room. "Where are your clothes, Miranda?"

"Upstairs."

She had not changed her position. Her head still drooped. She did not look at him.

"Perhaps you will get them for me," the man said. He was very tall. His head nearly touched the low beams of the ceiling. He spoke as if he were giving an order, without looking at me. When I came back down the stairs carrying her clothes rolled in a ball, he had taken her arm and led her to the door. Her head still drooped, the wet strands of dark hair shielding her face. She did not speak to me when they left, nor did he.

In the morning I found my orange dressing gown folded inside a box that had been placed on the stone doorstep already dried by the brilliance of the sun. Whoever had brought it there had come silently, for I had slept lightly since dawn, with the latticed windows thrown wide open. There was no note inside the box. It was strange, perhaps, that I had thought there might be when I opened it. I determined to put the incident of the night before out of my mind.

There was a great deal I wanted to do. The night before I had lain awake for a long time, pretending that it was the rain dripping from the thatch that kept me awake but knowing it was because I had been made to feel an interloper by Paul Randolph.

I was not, I knew, a striking woman, not the sort who automatically receives deference even from the worst sort of man. My fair hair was my only really good feature, and out of sheer carelessness I usually kept that knotted in a bun at the nape of my neck. My complexion was pale from too much living in sunless rooms, from too much walking of sunless streets. My eyes were simply blue, not azure or violet or any other such exotic shade that is so frequently applied to heroines in novels. Even my nose had no character, being what is usually called retroussé, and my mouth was simply full.

Obviously Paul Randolph was a man who appreciated beauty in women. His wife must have been a lovely woman when he married her. But even though my externals did not interest him, there had been no need for him to treat me as if I did not exist. That was a contradiction, of course. If I did not exist as far as he was concerned, I was no interloper. Miranda had disturbed me, but it was he who had taken the happiness away from the day, and into the reaches of the night it was he who had disturbed my peace of mind and made me toss in restless misery. I had tried to think of all the things I planned to do the next day, but it had been useless. Even my dreams, when I

finally fell asleep, were dark and menacing. When I
awoke, I was glad that I could not remember them.

But now with the bright sunlight glistening on the rain-
drenched grass and the leaves of the old oaks that surrounded the cottage, I could think with pleasure of the
immediate future. Violets were hidden in odd crannies of
the rough lawn, and wallflowers flaunted their bright
colors against the stone walls of the cottage.

The little house nestled in a hollow of land, surrounded
by trees and bushes. I knew that somewhere beyond the
rise of land to the north the sea must lie. Later I would
seek it out, but now I was simply glad that I was so well
hidden from the world. It had been too dark and foggy the
night before for me to know whether or not Pennarth was
visible from here, and I had held my breath as I had
stepped out into the morning sunlight, afraid that I would
find the house looming over me. But there was nothing to
see except a wilderness of trees, thickly leafed. Perhaps
when I walked to the gate, I would see someone, but I
doubted, from Paul Randolph's attitude, that they would
seek me out. As for Miranda, I was somehow certain she
would be discouraged from coming here again.

After I had breakfasted at the little table beside the
opened kitchen window, listening to the calling of the
birds outside, I cleaned the cottage thoroughly, knowing
that only when I had gone over it inch by inch with
dustcloth, scrub brush, and broom would I feel that it was
truly mine. As the dust disappeared, so did my uncertain-
ties, and I sang aloud as I worked, something I had not
done for years. Bed-sitters are no place for singing, and I
would never have to go back to them or to London.

When everything shone, I paused to eat a sandwich and
faced the question of what to do next. Clearly I would
have to deliver the car to Bertha and Greg at St. Ives, if
not today then by tomorrow. For all I knew, there might
be some objection to my having parked it where I had.
First, however, it would be only sensible to drive to the

village to get a month's supply of everything that was not perishable. As for what future arrangements I might make about groceries, I could see to that later.

Miranda had said that deliveries came to Pennarth once a week. Perhaps I could make some arrangement with the local stores to have my own orders brought out at the same time. But no. That might necessitate some contact with the Randolphs, and I was eager to avoid that. After all, the village could not be more than three or four miles away. It would do me good to walk that distance every day.

When I emerged from the path leading from the cottage to the gatehouse, there was no one in sight, and I paused for a moment to look across what seemed to be acres of roughly terraced land, broken by clumps of trees, to Pennarth. It was too far distant for me to be certain, but the house seemed to spring out of the rock that crowned the hill. To the north there seemed to be cliffs which dropped off sharply, I imagined, to the sea.

But the house itself claimed the eye completely. It was a grotesque building. To the south a wing mounted with round, sharply pointed towers formed a castle effect, but the main body of the structure was of a completely different style and period. Rectangular in shape, it was faced with ten long windows on each of its two floors, five on each side of a columned entrance topped with what appeared to be a sculptured pediment, the general effect being of a Greek temple. The stone of both the main building and the wing was gray and weather-stained, as though they had been constructed at the same time. It was an ugly building, made ominous even under a clear sky by the fact that the windows to the north had been bricked in, giving that section of the house a derelict air, whereas in the towered wing the windows, which were smaller and more numerous, appeared to be empty of glass, gaping like a toothless jaw.

I shivered in the warm sunlight, the touch of fear I had

felt the night before returning. And yet it was only a
house—a large manor house. England was full of them,
and many had been allowed to fall into ruins. I had heard
people say that it was impossible in these times to afford
the expense of maintaining such great houses. Miss Randolph's brother had no doubt been forced to allow the
tower wing to fall into disrepair.

Obviously the family must inhabit the section to the left
of the door, which was probably more room than they
needed if only Miranda and her husband and his father
lived there. It was logical to brick up windows in a section
of the house that was not being used. It may have been
done in the eighteenth century when the government had
experimented with a tax on windows; yet the brickwork
from this distance looked new. Miss Randolph had never
told me just how old Pennarth was.

All of that did not matter. I knew only that even to look
at it made me uneasy, as though it were, in some way, a
menacing presence. I turned my back on it and hurried to
the car. It started reluctantly, and I backed it around and
started for the village, determined, no matter how absurd
it sounded, not to look at Pennarth too often. When it was
out of sight, I could forget it. As long as I could avoid the
sight of it and avoid, as well, the people who lived in it, I
could be as happy as I wanted to be.

I drove slowly with the windows rolled down, savoring
the smell of salt in the warm air and the sheer beauty of a
day that could cast its magic even over the bare windswept
land to my right, an inhospitable land dotted here and
there with low stone cottages. Once I was in sight of the
sea, however, there was no need of sun or blue sky to
provide beauty. The fog had hidden that vast stretch of
ocean stretching to a distant horizon the night before, but
now I could see every white-capped wave, while against
the skyline a tramp steamer made its majestic way into the
open Atlantic, like a wooden model of a ship pulled across
a blue stage by invisible strings.

I suddenly came upon the village around a curve in a road high hedged with hawthorn. I had passed through it the afternoon before, but I noticed just a cluster of stone houses. Now I saw that one of them, the only one with whitewashed walls, was a grocery store and that across from it was a thatched-roof cottage much like my own, with a sign over the door that indicated it was a post office. Aside from a single gas pump that stood in front of another cottage, there seemed to be no other centers of commerce in the town. I stopped the car in front of the grocery store and went inside.

Obviously the partitions had been knocked out of the lower floor of an ordinary house to create the long room into which I stepped. A bell jangled over the door, and an old woman with a bundle of white hair piled high on her head appeared behind the counter. She greeted me and remained waiting silently as I gathered together what I thought might be enough canned goods to last me for the next four weeks and heaped beside them fresh fruit and vegetables and meat to the extent that I thought the tiny refrigerator at the cottage would hold. Expressionlessly the old woman added up the cost on a piece of white notebook paper. Only when I asked about deliveries did she look at me with awakened curiosity.

"And whereabouts would you be staying?" she asked, tucking the pencil in her hair and beginning to arrange the canned goods in a box that she pulled from beneath the counter.

"At the cottage on the Pennarth estate."

Her faded blue eyes sharpened. "You're the one from London, then?" she said. "The one Miss Lena had as a companion."

It was clear that there were no secrets in this isolated bit of country. I admitted that that was true.

"Miss Lena, now," the old woman said, "she was a fine woman. Not that we saw much of her about here after she went away to school. One of those girls' schools in the

east, it was. The Randolphs never sent their children to the
local school. It wasn't to be expected, them being what
they are."

"She came back here from time to time after that, didn't
she?" I said. It occurred to me that this woman and Miss
Randolph must have been much the same age. It was
strange, somehow, to meet someone who had been her
contemporary and find her still rosy-cheeked and in good
health. When Miss Randolph died, she had seemed to me
to take her generation with her, perhaps because she had
been the only old person I had ever known well, my own
grandparents having died when I was still a child.

"Back to the cottage, you mean," the old woman said
with a sly smile, which, for no reason, made me think of
Miranda. "Never to the big house, not after her mother
died, and then only for the funeral services. They held
them there, you know, in their own private chapel with no
proper clergy attending. Private folk, the Randolphs. Miss
Lena's brother, now, the last time I caught sight of him
must have been twenty-five years ago. A recluse, that's
what people call him. And there's others that have another
name for it." She took a deep breath, as though once
launched into garrulity, she did not know how to stop.
"And now his son coming to be just like him. But, then,
it's likely you'd know more about all that than I, you being
such a friend of Miss Lena's."

The temptation to linger on and gossip was almost irre-
sistible. Although the old woman kept on stacking cans in
the boxes, I could see that she was holding herself stiff
with anticipation. But I murmured something about Miss
Randolph being a fine woman and began to help her box
the groceries. After all, she was interested in gathering
some fresh information, and there was nothing I could tell
her, or would tell had I been able to. To gossip about the
people who lived at Pennarth would be tantamount to
involving myself in some slight way in their lives, and I
knew, after last night, that if anything could destroy the
peace of my new life, it would be such an involvement.

Instead I turned the conversation back to the subject of deliveries and learned that the store that provided for the Randolphs' domestic needs was located at Truro and that although the old woman's grandson made deliveries of meat and dairy goods on his bicycle to the house in the village, he would not be prepared to take care of my needs. The boy, a shock-haired lad of about fourteen, made his appearance in time to help me load the boxes into the car, and I drove away, reconciling myself to a walk of eight miles and seriously considering the possibility of stretching my slender funds to the point of purchasing a bicycle.

But it was strange how little the practical necessities of existence seemed to matter as I drove through the increasingly familiar countryside, the salty wind blowing my hair loose from its bun, the sea gulls swooping overhead uttering shrill screams, the estuary that I had not noticed before, its mud flats bared at low tide. Midway between horizon and land a sailboat drifted like a billowing white handkerchief across the stark blue of the sea. I had not felt as happy in years.

It was midafternoon by the time I carried the last of the groceries through the rusting gate down the path that led to the cottage. The tiny kitchen greeted me like an old friend, but I did not pause to put away anything except the perishables.

Hurrying across the stubbled grass of the side lawn, I made my way through a tangle of bushes and up the rise toward the pulsing sound of the sea. Emerging on a rocky ledge, I saw it stretched out before me. The sailboat was still there, bobbing about closer to land now, and I saw a man shifting the mainsail. I had a sudden impulse to call out to him and wave my arms from sheer exultation.

There was a cove below me, a tiny crescent of white sand. For a moment I did not see how it would ever be possible to get down to it from this point, since the ledge on which I was standing mounted a sheer drop of at least three hundred feet to the crashing surf. And then, to my right, I saw what looked to be a path leading down to the sand. Overgrown with brambles, it did not look like an easy way to take, but it was my only access, and I determined that I would use it.

I could see to my left the promontory on which Pennarth sat, although I could not see the house itself. If the people there ever came down to the sea, they certainly did not make use of this distant cove. It could be my own private place. Despite the breeze from the water, the air was warm. Below in the sun trap created by the sheltering cliffs it would be as hot as a summer's day. I turned back to the cottage to put on my bathing suit and sunbathe. I had made the cottage my own by cleaning it. I could make the cove my own, as well, by lying on the sand.

I was just opening the cottage door when I saw the man. He was standing by the hedge with a pair of gigantic clippers in his hand. Dressed as a workman, his striped trousers an obviously cast-off portion of what had once been a best suit, his brown sweater patched at the elbows and frayed about the cuffs, he stared at me with dark eyes set deep in a broad-boned, deeply tanned, and weathered face.

"I'm Ora Johnson," he muttered as I turned and came down the path toward him.

The name had a familiar ring, and I realized that it was the one I had written on the check Miss Randolph had sent once a year to the man who maintained the cottage for her.

"I come to find out if you'll be wanting anything done," he said, ducking his head awkwardly as I came close to him. "Now that Miss Lena's dead and all. . . ."

It was, I realized, the second time today I had heard Miss Randolph referred to in that way. It was understandable, perhaps, from the old woman who ran the grocery store in the village, since she had known the woman who had been my employer from the time she was a girl. But this man was younger, perhaps in his fifties, with a mass of gray hair and strong powerful shoulders and arms.

As I walked around the hedge to face him, he began squeezing the handle of the clippers together with no more effort than if they had been a pair of scissors. I knew he wanted to know whether or not I would want him to continue to keep the cottage in repair. The sum Miss Randolph had paid him yearly leaped to my mind. It had not been a great deal, but it was more than I could afford.

There was no need to introduce myself. Obviously he knew who I was, as did everyone else in the village. I smiled tentatively in the face of his scowl.

"Is there a lot to be done?" I asked.

"More than enough for what she paid me," he muttered. "There's this hedge to keep clipped and the yard to see to, and that there thatch on the roof is needing to be patched proper before the autumn. Not to speak of the trouble you'll be having with the drains."

"I'm afraid," I said, "that I won't be able to have anything done except what's absolutely necessary. Everything seems to be in working order now."

"That's as may be," he said, half turning from me so that I could not meet his eyes. "Likely you won't be staying long in any case."

"I intend to live here permanently," I told him.

He made a sound deep in his throat, which might have been an indication of disbelief.

" 'Tis a lonely place, this," he said. "Summers it's one thing, but winter's another."

It was, I knew, no use arguing with him. "I won't be able to afford any repairs that aren't absolutely necessary," I repeated. "In fact, I'll have to wait until something goes wrong and then see about putting it right. Perhaps if you'll let me know where I can find you if I need anything done. . . ."

"If you aren't wanting it done now, likely you won't later," he said, his head still turned away.

"Why do you think that?" I demanded.

"If it ain't the winter will drive you away, it's the old man up there," he muttered, gesturing with the clippers in the general direction of Pennarth. "If you don't know it now, you might as well. It was one thing when it was his sister, but it ain't likely that the old devil up there will let you stay."

2

I found Bertha and Greg living in one of those tiny whitewashed stone houses that tumble in rows down the steep narrow cobbled streets of St. Ives to the harbor. The back of the little house opened out unexpectedly onto a garden surrounded by a high stone wall. It was here that Bertha and I sat the next morning, sunning ourselves in deck chairs while Greg chipped away at an abstract figure of a woman that was slowly taking shape out of a huge block of gray-white granite.

"Do you really think, then," Bertha said briskly, setting her cup of tea on the grass beside her to cool, "that there's a chance you won't be allowed to keep the cottage?"

She was a tall, big-boned woman who would look the same in twenty years as she did now. Her brown hair was cut unstylishly in a straight bang across her broad forehead and clipped again just below her ears. Her face was plain but so mobile that when she spoke, she often seemed beautiful. The smock she was wearing, paint-spattered and frayed, might have been the same one she had worn when we were both in art school.

Nothing about her seemed to have changed, and I knew that although a year had passed since we had seen one another and that now the most important person in her life was the tall thin man with tousled red hair and a shaggy beard who muttered to himself as he chipped away at the mound of stone glittering in the sunlight, we could be as close as we had ever been. There would never be any possibility that my confidences might be a burden to her. As I realized that, a sudden sense of relief came over me.

"If there had been," I said, "I would have thought that Mr. Soleway would have given me some warning."

"Mr. Soleway?"

"Miss Randolph's solicitor. The man who told me that she had left me the cottage."

Bertha lit a cigarette and inhaled deeply. Her skin was deeply tanned and healthy. Beside her I felt pale and somehow like a weak reflection of what I might be. I wished that I had her drive, her determination. Even the way she was attacking my problem now was typical of the manner in which she always cut through incidentals to the crux of the matter.

"Did he give you any papers?" she asked me. "A deed, for example."

I shook my head. "He said there were certain legal technicalities——"

"Lawyer's jargon," Bertha interrupted scornfully. "Either the cottage is yours or it isn't. My advice to you would be to contact this Soleway chap as soon as possible and tell him what's going on."

"Nothing's going on really," I protested. "The fact that a village handyman thinks Mr. Randolph isn't going to let me stay there doesn't mean anything."

"And yet it upset you?"

I nodded. There was no use denying it. I had seen the dark circles under my eyes when I dressed to come here. Bertha knew me well enough to have guessed that the idea of any uncertainty in my life would have caused me to undergo a sleepless night.

"They must be peculiar people, these Randolphs," Bertha said reflectively. "You say that the daughter-in-law might be insane?"

"I don't know," I said. "She certainly didn't act like anyone else I've ever met. But living up there in that ghastly place might make anyone odd."

"People on the whole are dangerous enough," Bertha said distinctly. "Peculiar people are more dangerous than most. You never know which way they're going to leap, for one thing."

I smiled at her. Some people, I knew, were put off by her habit of making pronouncements, but I had never been one of them.

"And you say that the son didn't speak to you when he came to get his wife at the cottage?"

"He asked me to go upstairs and get her clothes," I said. "Or perhaps I ought to say that he ordered me."

"That's the only way that some men are able to convince themselves that they exist," Bertha said happily. "Not that what Paul Randolph is or is not needs to concern us. The fact that he or someone else left your dressing gown on the doorstep the next morning is a certain sign that the family, Miranda excepted, doesn't want to have anything to do with you."

"That doesn't matter to me," I assured her. "I didn't come expecting to have any contact with them. I don't believe Miss Randolph thought that would happen, either. She knew I wanted to be alone to paint. I doubt if she would have left me the cottage if she thought there would be any unpleasantness."

"But you told me she was well aware of her brother's desire that the entire estate be his."

"Yes, but apparently the few times she stayed at the cottage herself she wasn't disturbed by the family."

"How long ago was that?"

I shrugged. "I'm not certain. A long time ago."

"And at that time her brother lived at Pennarth alone?"

"I think so, yes. There must have been a wife at some time or other, because he has a son. But Miss Randolph never really told me about them. She didn't like to talk about them because it made her unhappy. She had no other family. She was a very lonely woman."

A doorbell rang, and Greg dropped his chisel and went into the house. Bertha was silent, staring thoughtfully at the wallflowers in the tiny path of garden. A girl laughed somewhere behind the wall, and I heard the roar of a motor as a car strained its way up the narrow street.

In the summer I knew the town would be packed with tourists. Even now I had noticed when I arrived a number of family groups, the fathers' faces red and blistering, mothers bedecked with broad-rimmed sun hats, the children straggling behind, happily licking ice pops. The shops had all seemed to be open, too, their low windows jammed with souvenirs. I had always thought that St. Ives must be too commercial a town for an artist to work in happily, although a good number of them did, but now I knew why Bertha and Greg loved the place.

They had only to step outside their front door to see the sea curling into the harbor, and there was the color and excitement of the village. Yet they still had the solitude they wanted for their work here in this garden and in the studio that composed the upper story of the house. And they had one another. For the first time since I had come to Cornwall it struck me that I might find myself lonely at times, and when I was, I determined not to wait too long before I came here.

"Of course," Bertha said, still concentrating on what I had told her, "if the situation were an ordinary one, you could simply go straight up to the house and get to know the family and find out if they intended to make any trouble. As things are, I would recommend a letter to Miss Randolph's solicitor to make your position quite clear. It's probable that there won't be any difficulties anyway. As you say, you're only going on Paul Randolph's unfriendliness and the word of a handyman. Probably the family will simply ignore you, and that will be that."

"I like to hear you say that," a man's voice announced. "*That* will be *that*. Somehow it seems to take care of everything."

He was young—about twenty-five—of medium height with wavy sun-bleached hair. He wore a paint-stained T-shirt and a pair of faded-blue dungarees. Tanned and smiling, he stood in the open doorway and grinned at us, Greg towering behind him. I felt an instant attraction to the stranger, perhaps because in the glow of sunlight he looked like a bronzed Apollo.

"Ron!" Bertha cried. "I'm glad you dropped by. Sara has a problem, and you may be able to help us. You know something about the Randolphs over at Pennarth, don't you?" She turned to me. "Ron's been here for years," she said. "He knows everything there is to know about this part of Cornwall."

That was the extent of the introductions. Neither Bertha nor Greg had ever been strong on formalities, but it seemed to satisfy the young man, for he dropped on the grass beside my deck chair and drank the tea from Bertha's cup.

"That's better," he said. "It's a thirsty day. Go on with whatever you're doing, Greg. You know I'd rather talk to two beautiful women than you any day."

He was the sort of person it was impossible not to like. I had met other young men like him in Greg's studio in London. They expected to be treated immediately like intimate friends, but in the end, if you did not demonstrate an absorbing interest in whatever they were painting or etching or sculpting, their interest waned. It was, perhaps, a characteristic peculiar to artists, and I had long since learned to respond warily to their apparent openness.

But Bertha did not ask him how his work was going, and he made no mention of it. I guessed from his T-shirt that he painted in oils. It was only when Bertha teasingly called him Mr. Farrow and asked him if he would like some more tea and a cup of his own that I realized with a shock of recognition that he must be the Ronald Farrow whose portraits of Cornish laborers had received much favorable comment at a one-man show last winter in London. I had attended the show in an effort to distract myself soon after Miss Randolph had died, and I remembered vividly the skill with which he had caught the dour dark Celtic quality of the men and women and children whose character and likeness he had transferred to canvas.

I would have said something of my admiration for what he had achieved, but he gave me no chance. With Bertha gone into the house and Greg chipping away tenderly again at the block of granite, the young man turned his attention on me.

"And what," he said, "would you be having to do with Pennarth? You aren't a Randolph, are you? With that hair and those eyes you certainly don't look it."

"You sound as if you do know them."

"I was born in the shadow of the wretched main house, you might say," Ron said lightly, leaning back on one elbow and staring up at me with the mischievous expression of a boy. "You've been to the village?"

"Yes. I bought groceries there yesterday."

"From old Mother Warren probably. Did she put you through the third degree?"

"She wanted to," I said, laughing, "but we both resisted the temptation to gossip. Why, is she a relative of yours?"

His face darkened. "No," he said abruptly. "I have no more relatives, as you call them." His smile returned as Bertha came back into the garden carrying a tray. "But friends are better, aren't they, Bertha?"

Obviously she did not know what he was talking about,

but she agreed. Then, pouring fresh tea for all of us, including Greg who drank his in a gulp and returned to his chipping, she reverted to what was, as far as she was concerned, the sole topic of conversation for the time being.

"Sara has been left old Miss Randolph's cottage," she said, sitting down on the edge of her deck chair and somehow giving the impression that she was about to conduct an official interrogation. "What used to be the gardener's house on the Pennarth estate."

Ron whistled softly. "How in God's name," he asked me, "did you manage that?"

Impatiently, as though an explanation from me might take too much time, Bertha told him. I sometimes thought she had missed her calling in not going into law. She could certainly have presented a summation par excellence.

"And how is old Mr. Randolph taking that?" Ron demanded. "I would have thought he would rather have had the cottage burned to the ground than to allow strangers on his precious land. When I was a boy, he kept mastiffs who would as soon have taken a leg off you as barked. They did maul a delivery boy once, and there was some question of a lawsuit. After that the dogs disappeared, and Randolph hired a couple of men from the village to patrol the place."

I explained about the present condition of the gate and the fact that no one had tried to keep me from entering the grounds.

"It's been so many years now that probably no one ever comes there anyway," Ron said thoughtfully. "No one in the village ever had any special liking for him. My father told me once that when Randolph was a young man, he used to organize hunts. That's not too usual in this part of the country, you know, and I take it he was more interested in doing whatever damage he could to the fields than he was in any quarry. Of course, you can't believe everything you hear, but he always sounded to me as though he were a particularly vicious man."

"I haven't seen or heard from him," I said.

"But she's met the son," Bertha added meaningfully.

"Paul?" Ron flung himself supine on the grass and stared up at us, his hands behind his head. "He's an odd one, too. When I was about eight, he used to come back now and then from Cambridge. There was money enough for him to have a car, God knows, but he always took the train as far as Exeter and hiked the rest of the way. The village made a big thing about that. It was all right for people like us to walk or take a bus, but one expected something better from the Randolphs. You don't mean he's come back to that pile permanently, do you? The last I heard he was in some sort of business in London. I never expected him to make the scene at Pennarth again after his sister died."

"His sister?" I stared at him, puzzled. Miss Randolph had never mentioned having a niece.

"I'm surprised you didn't hear about her," Ron muttered, closing his eyes against the glare of the sun. But he kept on talking, slowly, as though he were having difficulty remembering. "Her name was Eileen," he said, "and she killed herself about the time I went away to university."

"Killed herself?" Bertha's voice was sharp. For a moment there was silence except for the cry of a gull overhead and the chipping of Greg's chisel against the marble.

Ron opened his eyes and pushed himself into a sitting position. "They called it suicide at any rate," he said grimly, "and no one around that part of the country is likely to question what a Randolph says."

"Well," Bertha said impatiently, "go on."

"It doesn't matter," I said. "He doesn't have to talk about it."

"If there's going to be any trouble about the cottage," Bertha said, "you ought to know as much about the situation as possible."

"But what happened to her happened a long time ago," I protested, not certain why I felt a certain antipathy about hearing any more about the girl who had taken her own life except that somehow every additional bit of information I was given about the Randolphs seemed increasingly to involve me with their lives. All that I really wanted, after all, was to be left alone. I did not want to know them, and neither did I want to think about them.

"It wasn't all that long ago," Ron said. "Only ten years. She was a late child. Her mother was much younger than old Randolph. She died just after she was born. I never heard much about the mother. But Eileen was a wild one right from the moment she could get around by herself. She was about my age, and she used to run off and come down to the estuary and muck around in the mud with the rest of us of the lower orders."

I had been smoothing a blade of grass between my fingers, but the bitterness in his voice made me look at him in surprise.

"You say that she committed suicide," Bertha prompted him. Obviously the details of Eileen Randolph's earlier life did not interest her. Ron did not appear to hear. His eyes seemed to be focused on some point just to the right of the block of granite. Sensing something, Greg left off chipping and turned to look at his friend curiously.

"I remember once," Ron said slowly, "when we were both about twelve, we arranged to meet on one of the beaches that run along the bottom of the cliffs below Pennarth. It was autumn, and a gale was beginning to blow. But we took a good deal of pride, Eileen and I, in doing what we had planned to do, and damn the elements, or her family, or any other so-called absolute."

He paused for a moment, and we waited in the sunny garden, listening to the bees humming in the flowers. It did not matter now, I knew, whether I wanted to hear this or not. Obviously Ron was reliving the event. To have stopped him now would have been like waking a sleepwalker from his dream. Even Bertha said nothing.

"She was built like a boy, then," Ron went on quickly.

"Tall and thin, and she insisted on cropping her hair close to her head. She was dark, you know. Like her brother and her father and the rest of the damned clan."

Suddenly I remembered one of the portraits that had impressed me most at the showing of his work. The girl he had painted had been somehow different from his other subjects, more finely boned with sensitive, troubled dark eyes. Her dark hair had been cut like a boy's, and there had been a certain tentative quality in the tilt of her head, as though she were about to turn and run.

I had noticed the portrait particularly, not only because of the girl herself, but because the style seemed less developed than that demonstrated in the other paintings. Had he painted Eileen Randolph when they were both very young? Somehow I did not dare to ask him, perhaps because I did not want to disturb the intensity with which he was remembering her, perhaps for some other reason I did not want to admit even to myself. After all, I had known this man for only a few minutes. It was impossible that the twinge I felt should be jealousy.

"We had planned to take my father's dory out," he went on. "God knows I'd been around the sea enough to know that it was dangerous with a southeast wind blowing the way it was. But as I said, we made our plans, and we kept them. Even so I wasn't certain she could get away from the house. They kept her in the charge of a sort of governess then, some monster of a woman who was supposed to serve as her teacher and guard. However, Eileen was waiting on the strip of beach when I got there. I don't know how I managed to keep that dory from being swept against the rocks, but I did. She waded out to meet me, and I pulled her up over the side."

He shrugged. "I suppose it was a fool's stunt. We tried to make it back to the estuary, but the dory sprang a leak. We were out of sight of the house by that time, but her brother found us with his motor launch. He was home on a visit. He must have been about twenty-eight, but I thought of him as being the same age as my father.

"I won't forget the look on his face when he caught up with us. I don't think at first he had any intention of rescuing me. He drew up to the side and cut that damn great motor and hauled her into the launch. Kicking and screaming she was." Ron smiled. "I think she would rather have gone down with me than have let him take her that way. I'm pretty sure he was tempted to push off and let me take my chances, but in the end he told me to get into the launch, too, and I wasn't such a fool as to refuse, not with the water up to my ankles."

Leaning over, he took Bertha's pack of cigarettes, which had slid off the deck chair to the ground, and lit one.

"And that's the end of the story," he said heavily. "I don't know why I told it. It doesn't do any good to rake up the past. I didn't see her much after that, anyway. She was packed off to a girls' school in a hurry, and one year they sent her to Switzerland to be finished, or whatever the hell they call it. Once in a while when she'd come home for a visit, we'd meet. But she'd changed. She. . . ."

He broke off, grinding the unfinished cigarette into the grass. For a moment no one spoke, and then Bertha cleared her throat.

"How old was she when she died?" she asked.

"Eighteen." He stared up at her with a sort of blank anger. I would not have asked another question at that point, but Bertha was made of different stuff.

"Where did it happen?" she said. "Away? Or at Pennarth?"

"At Pennarth, of course. It was the place where she was most unhappy."

"And why——" Bertha began.

"No," I said. "It can't do any good asking that kind of question."

"Do you think I mind?" Ron demanded in a loud voice. His face was twisted and drawn. He did not bear any resemblance to the young man who a short while ago had stood grinning in the doorway. "Do you think any of this matters to me anymore? It's just an old story, and now

that you've heard this much of it, you might as well hear
the rest."

The sun was still shining, but I felt chilled. I hunched
myself in the deck chair and wrapped my arms around
myself.

"Eileen had been home for a while during summer vacation," Ron said in a strangled voice. "Every time she came
back she would manage to slip out, and we would meet
somewhere." He turned to me. "Do you want to know
where?"

I murmured something to the effect that it didn't matter,
but he did not appear to hear me. I had an absurd impulse
to protect him against his own memories. There was something about him that made me want to take care of him.
But we were only strangers. I had to remind myself of that
forceably. If he was determined to tell us about the past,
there was no way I could stop him.

"In the old gardener's cottage," he said. "Her aunt's
cottage. Your cottage. I discovered that I had a knack for
housebreaking. We got in through the boxroom window."

"Go on," Bertha urged steadily.

"She was home a few weeks, and then she went back to
her school. Then during the last week of October she came
back. It wasn't the end of the term, but she came back.
Her father owned a big gray Bentley then, and he had a
chauffeur. I saw her in it. She was looking straight ahead
at the road. I shouted at her, but she didn't look at me."

His face was stiff now, expressionless. "That was the
last time I saw her," he said. "I waited that night at the
cottage. And the next. The third night I didn't go. I was so
certain she could get away to see me if she wanted to. And
that night, the night I wasn't there, she came."

"How do you know?" Bertha said in a low voice. "How
do you know she came to the cottage if you weren't
there?"

"Because the next morning a fisherman found her body
at the bottom of the cliff," Ron said softly. "In the cove."

"But why?" I burst out involuntarily.

Ron rose to his feet and plunged his hands in the pockets of his dungarees, but not before I saw that his fingers were clenched as though he wanted to strike out at all of us.

"There were a good many rumors," he replied, keeping his voice even with an obvious effort. "You know what a village is. They said she was pregnant, that she was going to have a child. And if she was, that child must have been mine."

He turned to face us, his mouth twisted in a grotesque attempt to smile. "And so, you see, I do know a good deal about the Randolphs. Anytime you have any more questions, Miss Grey, you can come to me."

After Ron's departure I felt somehow awkward with Bertha. It was a blessing when lunch was over. Greg offered to drive me back to the cottage, wistfully looking over his shoulder at the block of granite. In the same breath he volunteered the information that there was a bus that ran to Land's End and must, consequently, pass Pennarth.

The look of relief on his face when I said I would rather poke around St. Ives for a while and then take the bus back to the cottage might have offended me if I had not known him so well. I left them with Bertha's reminder that I was to contact the solicitor in London and that they would expect to see me again soon.

At a bookstore I learned there was a bus at two and another at four, and I found that I was not eager to return to Pennarth immediately. I was not sure why I wanted to linger here in this picturesque but crowded little town. After all, I had come to Cornwall to paint, and the sooner I started, the sooner I would become absorbed in the only activity that could free me from my own thoughts.

I rationalized that I would not be able to come here often, that I was enjoying the colorful carnival aspects of a traditional English holiday spa, that there were certain art supplies I needed to buy. But as I descended the winding cobbled streets leading to the shops that fronted the harbor, all I could really think about was the story Ron had told us and the look on his face when he had described the circumstances of Eileen Randolph's death.

It was not strange, perhaps, that Miss Randolph had not told me the story, since she had told me so little about her family. But it was odd that she had never admitted the existence of a niece. And yet the story Ron had told had to be true. I wondered if the cottage would seem the same to me or whether both the house and the sandy cove below the cliff would be peopled by ghosts from this time on.

At ten minutes to four I was waiting outside the fish and chips shop where the bus was supposed to make its stop, my arms full of bundles. I stood, staring out at the glittering blue of the harbor, not really seeing it, my mind grappling with the intricacies of my meager finances. Adding up what I had spent on supplies yesterday and today, I could see that the remainder of the month must not involve any further major expenditures. I determined to spend my mornings and part of the afternoon painting and the remainder of my time reading, bathing, and tramping about the countryside. It was the sort of life I had sought for many years. Why was it, then, that I was scheduling my activities in my mind as compulsively as I had done in London? Shifting my packages in my arms, I determined that what I needed most was some time alone. After only a few hours with other people I found myself as highly strung as I had been living in the city.

I was so engrossed in my own thoughts that I did not notice the sports car that pulled up in front of me until a man spoke to me. I did not catch all the words, but it was clear that he was asking me if I wanted a ride. Irritated by the kind of intrusion on my privacy that I had expected to find only in London, I bent down awkwardly to articulate my refusal through the open window and found myself looking into the face of Paul Randolph.

Before I had a chance to speak, he leaned over and opened the door. The bus that had driven up behind him was being accelerated and stopped in an ominous manner as the driver, bent over the high wheel, stared down at us and muttered imprecations. Wordlessly, I handed in my packages and got into the car. In a moment we were whipping along the sea-front drive, headed out of town.

I had not really looked at him closely the night he had come to the cottage to take his wife back to Pennarth, and now I had to suppress the impulse to stare. He had been a menacing figure the night of the storm. Certainly not the sort of man I would have thought to own a white Jaguar and drive it at breakneck speeds down narrow lanes, as we were doing now.

His dark hair was ruffled by the wind from the open windows, and he was wearing old corduroy slacks and a blue sweater pushed up at the arms. His face in profile was that of a younger man than I knew him to be, and although he was not smiling, he looked less grim than the night he had ushered Miranda out of the cottage. There was about him, however, an atmosphere of tension.

"I suppose," he said, "I ought to apologize for my wife's behavior the other night."

"There's no need," I said. "She was caught in the rain and decided to wait in my car. It seemed the sensible thing for her to come back to the cottage with me."

"I suppose it was," he said, maneuvering the car at top speed around a hairpin turn. The moor opened out in front of us, and in the distance I saw the peak of one of the clay heaps that dotted the countryside. I considered asking him a question about the china-clay industry, if for no other reason than to divert the conversation from his wife. I had had enough discussion of the affairs of the Randolphs to last me for the day.

"However," he went on before I could speak, "if you knew my wife better, you would realize that I had good reason to be concerned."

I said nothing, and at the same moment we turned to

look at one another. In an instant I remembered the eyes of the girl in the portrait Ron had painted. These were the same eyes, dark and brooding.

Instantly he turned his attention back to the road. "And do you find the cottage comfortable?" he said. "I understand that that man Johnson has kept it in fairly decent repair."

"It's very comfortable," I said. It occurred to me that under ordinary circumstances the conversation would turn to his aunt. None of the family had written to me after her death, either to ask about her last illness or to indicate that they would attend the funeral. The only flowers to deck her casket had been a bouquet of roses I had ordered and a small bunch of spring flowers which had arrived with no card. Even if they had determined to forget her existence then, at least my presence ought to have made some comment about her unavoidable. But instead Paul Randolph was silent. He did not speak again until we reached the village.

"Do you plan to stay for the entire summer?" he asked me.

I felt a surge of anger. This, then, was the thin edge of the wedge. He was indicating to me quite clearly that the family did not expect me to remain long.

"I plan to stay there indefinitely," I replied.

Again he glanced at me, but this time I did not turn to meet his eyes. "It's rather isolated, surely," he said, "for a woman alone."

"I paint," I said shortly. "For some years I've been living and studying in London. I need to be alone to see if I can do the sort of thing I want to do."

He turned, and I met his eyes again, seeing the flash of interest in them. I told myself that I did not care what he thought of me, but at least I wanted him to know me for what I was. If he could comprehend that I was a serious artist, and not simply a scatterbrained young woman who had come to this remote part of England because of some romantic notions, something might have been gained.

We were passing the estuary now. The tide was rising, covering the ugliness of the mud flats. I found myself remembering what Ron had said about how he and this man's sister had played here as children over a decade ago. Did Ron, I wondered, ever come back? Or was St. Ives as close as he dared to return to what must be painful scenes?

"If you're an artist," Paul Randolph said slowly, "you must know people at St. Ives."

"A few," I said. I did not, I decided, want to answer any more questions. I had told him all it was necessary for him to know, that I had come here for a reason and that I intended to stay. I had accepted the ride because I had been taken by surprise and because it would have been churlish for me to have refused. But now I wanted to be back at the cottage, alone. And yet, for some ironic reason, he was not forcing the car as he had at first.

As we left the estuary behind us, we could not have been traveling more than thirty miles an hour, and I saw him shift down into third gear. To our right the sea glittered in the afternoon sun, and through the opened windows came the thick sweet smell of honeysuckle.

"Have you close friends there?" he asked me unexpectedly.

I was determined not to tell him any more than I had, although why it should matter if I mentioned Bertha and Greg by name I did not know. Still, I was reluctant to do so. And as for Ron, it was clear that I should say nothing about him. I was certain that this man would remember him, even if the last time he had seen Ron might have been on that stormy day when he had plucked him and Eileen from a sinking dory.

What was it Ron had said? That he thought if Paul Randolph had followed his own inclinations, he would have left him there to go down with the boat? Had the Randolphs, I wondered, known that the boy from the village had continued to see Eileen? That they had been lovers? It was, I knew, useless to make guesses. It had only been village rumor that she was pregnant when she died.

Even Ron could not be certain of that, even though it had been possible.

If she had been expecting a child, however, there were so many questions left unanswered. Was that the reason she had been taken out of school in the middle of a term? And once she was back at Pennarth, had she told them the truth about who had fathered the baby? What had her father's reaction been? Ron had implied that he was a vicious man. Certainly Miss Randolph had chosen to stay well away from him, even though he was her father.

It was absurd for me to have conceptualized him, but I had, I realized, without even knowing it. I could see him, bent and wrinkled, his face twisted in a mask of ugliness as he ceaselessly questioned a dark-eyed girl with hair cropped like a boy's, demanding to know who had been responsible for her condition, condemning her for the disgrace she had brought on the family, tormenting her until she had, in desperation, escaped that monstrous house and thrown herself from the cliffs.

I had forgotten the man beside me now, so caught up was I in my own imagining—forgotten the momentary reality of him, that is. For in my mind's eye I could see him standing in the background, listening to the weeping of the young girl who was his sister, knowing more, perhaps, than he would disclose. For he, at least, had known something of the closeness of her relationship with the boy from the village. Perhaps, over the years, he had detected more than a simple escapade in Ron's dory. Perhaps he had been aware of the meetings at the cottage and had said nothing. Perhaps by letting events take their natural course he had served his own purposes.

Suddenly I became conscious of the fact that the sports car was speeding ahead again in high gear, and I realized that I had made no answer to Paul Randolph's question. I felt my cheeks grow hot as though he might have been able to read my mind.

"Yes," I said belatedly. "I have two close friends in St. Ives."

He did not answer, and I could not blame him. As far as he knew I had snubbed him. We reached the vine-tangled gates to the estate, and he brought the car to an abrupt halt.

"You'll want to get out here," he said in an expressionless voice. "We no longer use this approach to the house. There's a road at the back that leads directly to the garages."

I started to remove my packages from behind the seat. He did not help me. His dark face was set as though he were deep in thought. Only when I awkwardly began to attempt to open the door did he speak.

"I don't want to keep you," he said, "but I think you ought to know that my father is rather upset about the terms of my aunt's will."

We were coming to the point then. This was why he had given me a ride. I did not want to hear what he had to say, but I knew that if I were not told now of what steps his father intended to take, I would be informed in some other way.

"Her solicitor told me I had been left the cottage outright," I said. "I'm sorry that your father is displeased, but you might as well tell him I intend to stay here."

"He'll be interested to hear of your determination to keep the place," Paul said without looking at me. "I think you may receive a letter from his own solicitor soon making you a very generous offer for it."

My first reaction was one of relief. If he hoped that I would sell the cottage, the old man must believe it was quite legally mine. What I had been afraid of was that there was some technicality on which he could simply take it away from me.

"I'm not interested in selling," I said. Then, in response to some sort of expansiveness which must have been born in the moment, I realized that legal action was not to be taken: "You can tell your father I quite understand that he might be wary about a total stranger coming to live here. But I *am* a serious artist. Tell him that. And I don't intend to invite a host of friends down from London for the weekends." I smiled. "Even if I had such a large collection of friends, I wouldn't invite them. As far as I'm concerned, he won't know that I'm here. I don't even have a car to clutter up the road."

I had been more effusive than I had meant to be, but the relief was so great that I had to react to it in some way. Paul Randolph was looking at me curiously.

"I'll admit," he said, "that you're not what I expected. About the car—what's happened to that?"

"It wasn't mine," I said and proceeded to explain about Greg and Bertha, something that, a few minutes ago, I would not have thought of doing.

As for the man beside me, he seemed to relax as I talked. His face grew less grim, and it was possible to forget that when I first met him, I had hated him. As he got out of the car and came around to open the door for me, it was possible for me to rationalize his rudeness on the night of the storm. His wife was obviously an unpredictable woman. He had good reason to be worried about her safety when she had not returned to the house. It was only natural that he had reacted as he had when he found her in the sitting room of my cottage, dressed incongruously in a dressing gown three sizes too small for her. Simple embarrassment could have made him so abrupt. Whatever the reasons for his behavior, it wouldn't hurt me to be friendly.

I got out of the car and waited as he leaned inside and brought out the packages.

"Perhaps I should help you. . . ." he began.

"No, there's no need. It was good of you to give me a lift." And then, afraid that he would think I was snubbing him again, I groped for something light to say. "You said I wasn't what you had expected," I said. "What sort of person did you think might be coming here?"

I had asked the wrong question. I knew that even before he answered me. His dark eyes seemed to mock both of us as he pushed open the rusting gate to let me pass. "We expected the sort of woman who would have been willing to invest three years of her life in a gamble," he said coolly. "Three years of acting the role of dedicated companion in return for a rather valuable bit of property."

"That cottage!" I exclaimed, outraged and bewildered at the same time. How did he dare to imply that I had been kind to his aunt only because I had wanted something from her?

"Yes, that cottage," Paul repeated. "In itself it's not worth much, perhaps. But a clever girl—and we were certain that you were a clever girl—might have figured out that my father would be willing to pay five times its real value to bring that part of the estate back into the family."

His meaning had been perfectly clear. It would be a long time before I forgot the icy quality of his smile as I pushed past him and hurried away down the path leading to the cottage. I was too angry to say then what I ought to have said. Still trembling with rage, I curled on the big bed in the attic room with motes of sunlight thick on the counterpane and promised myself that I would never speak to the man again, let alone set eyes on him if I could help it.

It would have been one thing if he had come straight out with what he had obviously intended to say from the start. Instead he pretended curiosity about my intentions. He tried to trick me into saying that I was interested in selling the cottage. When I failed to nibble at the bait, he pretended to believe I really meant to live here indefinitely. But he was certain all along that his preconceived notions about me were true. He said that he had been wrong about me. How amused he must have been when I finally responded to his apparent friendliness. And then when he knew that I was no longer expecting an attack, he struck out. I had seen the look in his eyes as he opened the gate for me, and I understood that although he had pretended blackmail was an idea of the past, he was actually warning me that he knew I was everything he and his father had assumed me to be and that my pretense of being someone quite different had simply amused him.

Throwing myself back against the pillows, I stared at the ceiling. My packages and the art supplies I had brought from London were still piled in a heap in a corner near the north window. I knew I should be unpacking them, since tomorrow there would be no excuse not to get to work. Or perhaps it would be better not to concentrate on finishing the still life I had been working on in London, but instead to take my sketch pad down to the cove in the morning and. . . .

It was no good. I could not concentrate on my work. The realization that Paul Randolph thought I was capable of having served as his aunt's companion for three years simply so that I could come into possession of this cottage infuriated me. I had never been able to bear having anyone think something about me that was not true. What kind of monster would I have to be to pretend to be an old woman's friend for so long with no other motive than that of greed? The fact that he could think such a thing about me was a measure of the sort of man he must be. Perhaps greed had brought him back to this place and kept him here.

As far as I knew, now that his sister was dead, there was no other possible heir to Pennarth, but he might have reason to fear that his father would change his will. Had he remained here, year after year, giving up a career and any sort of variety in life simply to protect his own interests? Was that why he was so certain that I had played the same role with his aunt?

I rolled over, pressing my face deep into the pillow, my fingers gripping the casing. In the first place what he suspected was absurd. I had had no idea, until the final days of her life, that Miss Randolph had any intentions of leaving me the cottage. It had never occurred to me that I might someday live and work in this lovely place. Even if she had made her decision earlier and had told me of it, it would have had no bearing on my staying with her. I had taken the position of companion out of desperation, yes, at a moment when I could find no other job that would leave me either the energy or the time to paint, but I stayed because I had learned to love her. The sum she paid me every month had been no more than enough, when added to the allowance from the trust fund my father had left me, to keep me alive and housed in London.

Once, a year before she died, I had had an opportunity to help with the restoration of some eighteenth-century wall paintings in a manor house in Kent. But by that time she was so ill that she was unable to cope even for a few days by herself. I had never told her of the opportunity I had turned down, and I had not considered myself a martyr in staying with her. There had been too few people to love in my life.

However, I knew that if I told Paul Randolph all this, he would interpret it to mean only that I had taken the job because I was desperate for money in the first place and that once she became really ill, I had stayed with his aunt for the purpose of turning vulture after her death.

How I hated him! Rolling off the bed, I pulled off the full skirt and peasant blouse I had worn into St. Ives and got out a pair of worn denim shorts and a pale-blue shirt. Peering at my face in the one small mirror over the rickety bureau, I tried to see myself as Paul had seen me, damning my pale plain oval of a face. There was nothing about my looks to support his concept of me. With my hair hanging loose about my shoulders I looked too simple, too bland, too childlike to be capable of the enormities he wanted to attribute to me. If I were to be a villain, why could I not at least look the part?

I went to the end of the room, intending to force myself to begin to unpack my easel. I found myself staring out the wide window to where the tip of the green hill beside the house touched the sky. It was odd that nowhere from the cottage could one see the nearby ocean. There might as well have been rolling meadows below that grassy promontory instead of white-flecked waves. Yet when I opened one of the casements, I could hear the roll of the surf.

Suddenly it was as though my ears and eyes were not mine but those of the old woman who had been my benefactor. She had been much younger when she had last been here, but time did not really matter. How many times had she stood where I was standing and listened to that unending roar? How many times had her eyes picked out the white clusters of violets on the slope? And had she, as she stood where I was standing, been a prey to the same sort of hatred that surged inside me now? Whatever the nature of her quarrel with her brother, there must have been an ugliness about it to have kept her from him for nearly half a century. Had she come here seeking peace and the memories of childhood and found only bitterness? I had never really known what bitterness was until now. It seemed to press heavily upon me like some tangible thing.

I picked up one of the packages I had brought from St. Ives and then, with the string partly undone, put it down again. There were too many ghosts in this long, low-ceilinged attic room. For a moment the ghost of Miss Randolph was pushed aside by that of an eager girl, turning into the arms of a boy with flaxen hair. They had been happy in this room, but I could not feel their happiness. They had left behind them only the atmosphere of hatred and fear, the miasma of guilty secrecy. Suddenly I found myself running down the narrow stairs and out the door into the sunlight, as though I were escaping something.

I took along a bottle of cheap rosé I had bought in the village. As the shadows fell, I sat on a narrow stretch of sand, which was all that was left of the cove at high tide, hugging my knees against the crispness of the rising sea breeze and trying to scoff at my own lunacy in ever imagining that I could make the place my own in any real sense.

True, I had made my way down the steep path that led to the sand, letting the brambles tear at my ankles. True, I had found a sheltered corner under a shelf of granite that I knew I would come to again and again, just as one marks a certain chair for one's own. But the cove, as well as the cottage, had been a part of other people's lives, and I would never be really unaware of their presence. Every night as I lay in my bed under the sloping eaves, I would think of a dark-eyed girl lying in a boy's arms. And whenever I came here, the image of that girl's crumpled body sprawled in the sand would be more real than the salt spray and the crying of the gulls overhead.

The moon rose, and the wind grew colder, and still I did not move. There was a little wine left, and I finished it. I leaned back against the rocks and closed my eyes, and suddenly I seemed to be running through a thick stand of trees, the low branches tearing at my clothes like clutching hands. Then I was beyond the trees, and the cottage lay before me, caught in the glow of moonlight, but the moon was not the moon I had seen rising over the sea like a thin horn of gold; it was a huge red autumn moon which seemed to swell until it filled the sky.

I heard myself calling a name. What name? My ears almost caught it before the sound faded into the echoless night. I called again, and again I could not hear. No one came. Despair twisted and curled inside me until I began to run again—past the cottage—as though I were running away from someone. Yes, there was someone behind me. Now the despair turned to fear, and I stood on the tip of the rise and saw the rocks plunging into the darkness of the sea, and the moon seemed to swell and swell until everything was a blood red.

I turned and saw the shadow of a man coming toward me—red shadow with its arms outstretched. I took one step back and then another, and stepped into nothingness. I screamed as I fell, and I awoke still screaming. The rocks were sharp against my head, and the water was lapping close to where I sat. The blood-red moon was replaced by a twist of silver in a star-flecked sky, and my cry of terror faded with the dream. Stiff and cold, I climbed back up the cliff and into the cottage. Without turning on a light I made my way up the narrow stairs and flung myself across the bed. This time when I slept, there were no dreams.

3

When I first saw the old man coming down the path toward the cottage the next morning, I had the conviction that it was Paul's father. But standing by the kitchen window, a cup of tea in my hand, I watched him for only a few minutes before I was certain that it could not be he, since nothing about him conformed with my preconceived image of the owner of Pennarth. His body gnarled, he hobbled along slowly, not, I thought, because he could not have walked faster, but because he did not want to. He carried a knotted stick in his hand, and every few feet he stopped and poked about in the bushes in a way that I had seen small boys do when they are looking for bird nests.

As he approached the hedge that surrounded the cottage, a squirrel ran chattering across the path in front of him. The old man remained where he was, staring up awkwardly into one of the beech-trees, apparently listening to the scolding of the small animal. Whatever the stranger's identity, I was determined to greet him as if his visit were an ordinary thing. The emotional crises of yesterday had all resulted from my contact with other people. It would be easy, I had decided as I lingered over breakfast, to put too much value on being alone and as a consequence, find that I could no longer cope with the ordinary wear and tear of personal relationships. Even if this man were Mr. Randolph, even if he had come here to ask me to leave, I intended to remain calm. But I was certain, somehow, that the owner of Pennarth would never wander down a lane in a shabby tweed suit and cap, beating at bushes with a stick and listening to the chatter of a squirrel.

The sunlight blinded me when I first walked out onto the stone doorstep, but then I saw the stranger standing at the foot of the path, staring at me with faded-blue eyes that were nearly hidden by a mop of white hair of a thickness and length that would have better suited a young man in university than someone so obviously an octogenarian.

"Squirrels now," he said, breathing heavily, "they're curious creatures. It's a mistake to think you can tame them, because you can't. They're as apt to turn vicious as snakes. That's what I tried to tell Lena when she insisted on putting crumbs and other bits and pieces out for them. 'It's not just that you can't trust them,' I told her, 'you'll be teaching them bad habits. What will they do in the autumn, when you're gone back to the city and they have to scrounge around for themselves for food? What you've got to do is remember they're wild animals, and so they should be treated.'"

His wrinkled red face puckered like a persimmon when he smiled. I had only the most general idea of what he was talking about, and it was not at all clear whether he was advising me or someone else, but I knew that he was a delight. I put out my hand to him and folded the dry fingers between my own. He grinned at me with toothless impishness.

"Now, that's what I like," he wheezed. "A girl who comes more than halfway and gives you a smile even though she don't know who the devil you are. You ought to be more careful with old men like myself, my dear. We're as wild as those squirrels at the core, and we'd as soon kiss a cheek as shake a hand any day."

I laughed, and he with me. In the tree the squirrel kept on scolding, and I felt that the cold dread of the night before could really be forgotten. There were no ghosts about today. I pulled a striped deck chair into the shade and dropped on the grass at the feet of the old man. He lowered himself into the seat with a good many grunts and groans, some of them, I felt certain, perfectly unnecessary but part of the role he had assigned himself. For although he was obviously in his eighties, there was something about him that gave the impression he was really a boy, acting with relish an assignment that life had forced on him.

"Now," he said when he was settled, "how would you like to guess who I am, my dear?"

I shook my head, still smiling. There was something about this old man that seemed to make it impossible for me to do anything but smile. I would have liked to humor him and make a guess. It seemed impossible that he could be Mr. Randolph. The quality of the tweed he was wearing, as well as his accent, made it clear that he was not one of the servants. He might be someone who lived between Pennarth and the village and who had decided to walk out to visit me. Still, bent as he was, I did not think that he could have walked far.

"I gave you a clue," he said, spreading his knees and bracing the walking stick on the ground between his feet. The boots he was wearing were, I noted, old-fashioned and high cut with inserts of elastic in the sides, but they were new boots and obviously handmade of the finest calfskin. "Yes," he said, "I gave you a clue when I was talking about the squirrel."

He was obviously so eager that I should make a correct

guess that I forced my mind back to what he had said—something about feeding squirrels. He had mentioned someone who insisted on feeding them anyway. Someone. A familiar name. Lena. Miss Randolph's name was Lena. Surely he could not have meant. . . .

"Then you must be her brother," I said, my smile fading. I did not want him to be Mr. Randolph, because if he were, then all of this charm could be nothing but a facade.

Old Mr. Randolph was a vicious man who, when he was young, had run with the hounds across the fields of cottagers, not caring about the damage he was causing. Mr. Randolph had entered into a quarrel with his sister which had hurt her so much that she had never been able to mention it to me. The owner of Pennarth was the sort of man who had kept his daughter captive, isolated from other children of her own age, without even trying to provide her with the understanding and love that she needed. A young girl who was really loved would never have thrown herself from the cliff. All the horror of the nightmare of the night before came back to me, and I pushed myself to my feet, hoping that the simple black slacks and jersey I had put on that morning gave me some sort of dignity. "You must be Mr. Randolph," I said.

The old man pulled in his chin like a turtle until it touched the brown knitted scarf he was wearing knotted about his throat. He considered me benevolently. "No," he said, "Herbert Randolph I am not, nor shall I ever be. And, I'm thinking, my dear, that it's a good thing I am not, from the look in your eyes. Do you know the fellow, then, that you have reason to hate him so?"

"No," I admitted, "and of course I don't really hate——"

"Ah, but you do, my dear!" The cherubic old man leaned forward with an effort and reached his hand up to mine. "And now," he said, "we will stop playing games, and you will sit down as you were sitting at my feet. As Lena used to do. And later you will make me tea."

I did as he told me and waited until he had settled

himself back against the sloping chair. For a moment it was very quiet, and there was no movement except the breeze brushing against his thick white hair. He had mentioned Miss Randolph again by her first name, which must mean that they had been close friends. He was about her age. I sensed somehow that he was disappointed because I had not guessed his name immediately, but Miss Randolph had given me the impression in the little that she had ever said about this place that she had maintained no acquaintances. Was she, I wondered, as a girl, as isolated from the villagers as her niece, Eileen, had been?

Surely this man had never lived in the village. He was the sort of old man who would have seemed quite at home walking in Kensington Gardens wearing a bowler and old school tie, and had it not been for the conscientious effort that he had made in the wearing of tweeds, he would have seemed out of place here. I wanted to ask him where and when he had known Miss Randolph, but I sensed that he preferred to direct the action of this encounter.

"My name," he said suddenly in a thunderous voice that made a robin close to us abandon the worm it was pulling out of the grass, "is Enoch Lessing. There now, my girl! That rings a bell, doesn't it?"

I wished desperately that I could tell him it did. Obviously he knew who I was and probably the capacity in which I had known Lena Randolph. Obviously, too, he had been close enough to her at one time or another to expect her to have mentioned him to me. I suddenly thought of the unmarked bouquet of spring flowers that had arrived just in time for her funeral.

"You sent the tulips and the daffodils," I said in a low voice.

He had been smiling, but when I said that, his face quite suddenly was caught in a distortion of intense sorrow. "I wanted to come," he said in a low voice, "but, then, it would have done no good. It wouldn't have brought her back, would it? It's odd, you know, I always thought I

would go before her. Men generally do. It's one of the few
advantages of being a man. So many old women. Reading
the obituary list every morning. I'm glad that it didn't have
to be like that for her. It's an awful thing, my dear, to lose
your friends one by one, but it's even worse when they're
all gone, and you see that the grim reaper is starting on the
next generation. Ah, Lena dead, and it seems only yesterday. . . . D'you know, my dear, I think I wouldn't mind
having that cup of tea now."

He made the request with heartiness, but while I was in
the kitchen waiting for the kettle to boil, I saw from the
window that he was rubbing his knotted fingers across his
eyes. When I came out carrying the tray, he was smiling
impishly again.

"Ah, that's better, my dear!" he wheezed, draining his
cup and holding it out for more. I had put a few lady-
fingers on a plate, and he took one of them and ate it
down at once, licking his fingers greedily. Again I was
aware of the strange impression that he was really a little
boy masquerading as an old man. Oddly enough the
thought made me want to cry.

"Now," he went on, "first things first. It was foolish of
me to expect that Lena might have mentioned me to you.
You were a very good friend to her, I know, because she
often told me so, but of course that doesn't mean that she
would tell you everything about her life."

"But how could she have told you about me?" I protested. "In the three years I was her companion, she never
had a single visitor that I was told about. Or saw. And I
was with her most of every day."

"No, no. You're quite right, my dear. I've not been up
to London for a good many years now, although there was
the time when I would have laughed at anyone who had
tried to tell me that I should ever live anywhere else. No, I
haven't seen Lena for a good many years. But we corresponded, you know—every day of our lives for the past
forty-eight years. What do you think of that now? If you
disbelieve me, I can show you the letters.

"When we began, we promised to keep them in note-books. Matching brown leather notebooks. I bought the first set at Harrods. She was living down here at Pennarth then. I was the one to be in London. And as I say, when I was a young sprout, you couldn't have told me I would ever hide myself away in the country like this. It's a fine county, Cornwall, and all that, but there's not much vari-ety. That's what I told my family the first time I went back to London on holiday after taking the job here. 'The sea and the moors are all very well,' I said, 'but one wouldn't want to make a full meal on them, would one?' Which makes me a fool, I guess."

I stared at him totally confused. The only thing clear to me was that he was claiming he and Miss Randolph had communicated by letter every day for an incredibly long time. And yet I could have sworn that she had never mentioned his name. As for the letters, I could not offer proof on that, one way or the other, since although I had brought her mail up to her flat every morning when I arrived, I had never glanced through it.

One thing, however, I did remember. That was the night she had discovered she would have to go to the hospital. The doctor had been frank with her. He had told her the stroke she had suffered would doubtlessly be repeated. He had shown her her death warrant that afternoon, and she had taken the news heroically. I was to stay with her that night, as I had stayed since the first attack crippled her legs.

After the doctor left, she asked me to build up the fire and to bring her the small steamer trunk kept under her bed. The key to the trunk was kept on a chain around her neck, and I unlocked it for her and put it on a low table beside her wheelchair.

Afterward, I sat, pretending to read, while she took one letter after another from the trunk, smoothed it between her fingers, and threw it on the coals. At first she stopped to read them, and looking at her surreptitiously, I saw her face grow soft and thoughtful as she scanned the words.

But after a while she grew tired and asked me to burn the rest. I did so, the flames scalding the tears that streamed down my face. If she realized I was crying, she gave no sign. By the time I finished, she was asleep, her head pressed back against the cushions of the chair, a faint smile on her lips. Perhaps she had realized, better than I, that one does not destroy the past by committing paper to fire.

"She burned the letters," I said in a low voice, twisting a blade of grass about my finger.

"I suppose that was the only thing to do," the old man murmured heavily. "My time will come soon, I suppose, although I don't think I could bear to destroy anything of hers. Even her letters. Tell me, my dear, did she suffer a great deal in the end? My last letter from her was written from the hospital the day before she died. She tried to sound gay, as though it were only a temporary thing, her being there. But of course I knew. I wanted to come to her, but she said No. Lena was a hard woman in many ways. I suppose most women are harder than men when it comes down to the important things. Do you know, every time I opened one of those last letters, I was afraid she would tell me that she was in pain. I've always been a coward about such things, my dear. Most men are. Don't let them tell you differently. But if you understand me, I could have stood the pain myself, but the thought of her. . . ."

"She went quite quietly," I said. "In her sleep."

"Ah!" For a moment the faded-blue eyes focused hard on the stick in his hand, as though he were willing himself to show no emotion. "We had good times, Lena and I. Strange, isn't it? It hurt a bit finding out that she hadn't mentioned me to you. 'You're a child in a good many ways, Enoch,' she used to say to me." His round face wrinkled puckishly in a grin under the thatch of white hair. "And she was right. I've made a good many mistakes in my lifetime from pure foolishness. I never should have stayed here, for one thing. Fancied myself a gentleman here, you see. Afraid that if I went back to London, I'd have to see myself for what I was."

He leaned forward, wheezing gently, until his pink face was very close to mine. "I'll tell you this, my dear," he said, "you'll be making a mistake if you linger here for long."

"It's very beautiful," I murmured. I did not know quite how to deal with him, how to react. It was not much help not knowing what place he had at Pennarth. For I was sure now that that was where he lived, although I could not have said why. I could have asked him, but somehow it seemed as though the question would be too abrupt, too exacting for an old man who obviously approached life obliquely.

"I suppose it is beautiful enough," he said now, looking up at the sunlight that filtered through the leaves of the old beech, "but I never really saw it as lovely as it is after she left. It takes courage, my girl, to leave the safe places behind us. When it's time, you'll know that. I can see that in your face. Character, that's what you have. Like Lena." His face puckered in a smile. "You don't need an old man like me to tell you about courage."

When I saw that he was trying to hoist himself out of the low chair, I rose and took his arm. I did not want to let him go without finding out more about him and why he had come here. He had warned me against staying here too long, but it had not been a threat. As he started down the path, leaning heavily on the stick, I searched for the right words. There had been a quality about our encounter that I did not want to change.

"Yesterday," I said, "I saw Paul Randolph."

The old man stopped and began to chuckle. "It's a good thing you said that, my dear," he said gleefully. "There's them who wouldn't be too pleased if I had come back with the message undelivered. But I'll tell you a pretty girl always did drive all the sense straight out of me."

"A message?"

"Aye, from the grand potentate himself."

I stared at him bewildered. "Do you mean Mr. Randolph?"

"The elder Mr. Randolph," Enoch Lessing said with a broad wink. "He wants to see you. That's it in a nutshell. This afternoon at four, he said, if it's convenient. Now, there's no need for you to frown, my girl. His bark's worse than his bite, no matter what Lena might have told you. But take an old man's advice. Don't say you won't come." Tilting his head, he peered at me anxiously. "He's a man as doesn't want to be crossed. Play the game his way, my dear. That way there'll be no trouble. And no matter what you think, trouble's the one thing we can all of us do without."

At four o'clock that afternoon I stood in what I supposed must be called the great hall of Pennarth, waiting for the middle-aged servant who had answered the door to take the message of my arrival to the man she had expressionlessly called the master. Because of the ruined tower that had appeared in an even more skeletal form as I approached it and the wing with the bricked-up windows, I had not known what I could expect to find inside the main body of the house. But the inhabited portion of Pennarth had obviously been kept as it had been when there were still vast amounts of money to expend on it.

The hall was huge, with paneled walls rising to the height of an ordinary ceiling. Above the paneling the walls were of stone buttressed by arches, which pushed themselves against a high half-timbered ceiling. Above me to the right of the door was a minstrel's gallery, fronted by an elaborately carved oak screen which once had shielded the eyes of those who had dined here from the musicians who played while they ate. There was no longer a long refectory table running the length of the hall. The stone floor was carpeted with Persian rugs, and two upholstered sofas of relatively modern design were placed at each side of the huge hooded fireplace. There were a few rather shabby occasional chairs dotting the rest of the room and a small gate-legged table in the center on which was set a vase full of spring flowers. The general atmosphere was one of neglect, as though the hall were never used except as a place to pass through.

I had not wanted to come. If the message had been brought to me in any other way, by anyone other than Enoch Lessing, I would have refused. As it had been, the old man did not wait for an answer. He hobbled off down the path with a final impish smile of farewell, as though he were certain of my reply.

Afterward, of course, I was sorry that I had not had the courage to send him back with a refusal. As the sky clouded over and the hours of the early afternoon passed, I had sat on the grassy knoll overlooking the sea with an untouched sketch pad beside me and cursed myself for having allowed still another day of my life here to be interrupted by an encounter that could not help being disturbing in some way.

It was not that I minded seeing Miranda once more, for all her mad ways. In a sense I would be relieved if she were present when I talked to her father-in-law. But I certainly did not want to see Paul Randolph again. As for Enoch, his position in the household was obscure. He had loved Lena Randolph. That much was clear. But what he had been doing in this place for so many years was not at all apparent. I had liked him immensely, but in a way he threatened me by suggesting that unless I came here to talk to the owner of Pennarth, there would be trouble of some sort. It seemed too much to hope, under the circumstances, that I had been invited to tea as an ordinary gesture of friendliness.

But as I walked through the mist up the broad unkempt gravel road that twisted its way to the house, I rationalized that this one interview was unavoidable and that once having met my antagonist, I would at least know his intentions as far as the cottage was concerned. If he appeared to take some legal steps against me, I would do as Bertha had advised and write to the solicitor in London, and then if I found that the cottage was truly and unchangeably mine, I would refuse all further contact with the old man.

Hearing the sound of steps on the stairs leading up to a wide doorway at the farther end of the room, I turned, my heart pounding. It was all very well for me to pretend to myself that I could cope with this visit without losing my self-possession, but I knew I was taut with nervousness. And then I saw Miranda standing in the doorway smiling at me.

In the context of this huge hall she did not seem as tall as she had in my cottage, but her appearance was almost as wild as it had been that night. Her dark hair was caught up at the top of her head in an untidy cluster of curls, and her face was so white that it looked as if it had been chalked. She was wearing a scarlet silk robe cut in an Oriental manner with slits up the side and with an elaborate dragon embroidered on the front. She came toward me, half running, a strangely exotic figure in the dim vastness of the room.

"I'm so glad you came!" she cried, clutching both my hands and swinging them back and forth. "I didn't think you would. I certainly wouldn't have come if I were you. But I should have known that you were brave enough to face him."

She began pulling me toward the stairs. "Come along," she said gaily. "I told Margaret I'd take you to the library myself. That's where he's going to see you. I heard him tell Paul that he would talk to you in the library. But he'll make you wait, you know. He won't come right away. He always makes people wait. It makes him feel important, I expect. But I knew you wouldn't mind so much if we had tea. He wouldn't think of giving you tea, of course. He never does. Oh, I'm so glad you came. We can have a lovely talk."

The stairs led up to a landing and then, bending, up again to a shadowy corridor paneled with dark wood. Miranda went ahead of me, tugging impatiently at my hand, leading me through another door and into a long high-ceilinged room lined with books.

"There!" Miranda said triumphantly, twisting my hand behind me as she turned back to shut the door. "Isn't this nice? Do you know this is the first time I've been in this room? Paul's father would hate it if he knew. He doesn't like me to touch his things."

My relief at having seen a familiar face was twisted with anxiety as soon as she said that. She bewildered me, as she had the other night, and I remembered that she had responded best when I had treated her as I would a child.

"It's a very nice room," I said in a low voice, "but I'm sure there are others just as nice. Don't you think we should wait somewhere else?"

Instantly her face fell into haggard lines. "No," she said petulantly. "I don't want to do that. Don't you think I won't hear him coming? Because I will, you know. I have very sharp ears. And when I hear him, I'll just hide in that closet over there. Don't you see?" she added. "If I hide there, I can hear everything he says to you."

Helplessly I detached my hand from hers and stared around the dusky room. The only light came from two wide windows to my right—windows that looked out into the gathering mist. But I could see enough to know that the only unusual thing about the room was the extraordinary orderliness with which everything was arranged. The books that lined the walls seemed to have been put in place according to size rather than any particular cataloguing system. An ornately carved desk was placed in the exact center of the room. Its top was completely bare except for a morocco-bound blotter. Facing the desk was a long leather couch flanked by two straight-backed chairs. It was a perfectly ordinary room, I suppose, but there was something about the absolute symmetry with which everything was arranged that created an ominous atmosphere.

"I don't think," I said to Miranda, "that hiding in the closet would be a very good idea. Besides, I can't think that your father-in-law will have anything very interesting to say to me."

With one of those mercurial changes of mood Miranda clapped her hands delightedly. The slender, slightly wrinkled fingers were, I saw, covered with rings which, if the size of the stones was any indication, could not possibly be anything but costume jewelry. "You're wrong!" she crowed. "I know part of what he's going to say to you already. I heard him telling Paul. Oh," she went on, leaning toward me and arching her penciled eyebrows high, "he's a horrible old man. A perfectly horrible old man."

I realized I could question her and perhaps be better prepared to meet the conditions of the interview, but that would have been somewhat like questioning a child about something he was not meant to overhear. More than that, I did not want to become the confidante of this woman, whose behavior was, to say the least, erratic. I found myself wishing that I had refused to come up to this room with her, that I had remained in the great hall waiting for the servant to return.

My meeting with the elder Mr. Randolph would undoubtedly be difficult enough without my bearing the burden of the knowledge that she was hiding in a closet, listening to what was said. I sank down on the arm of the leather sofa and watched Miranda as she began to pace restlessly back and forth across the room, her scarlet robe billowing about her tall figure as she turned.

"Martha should have brought tea by now," she muttered. "We won't have time if she doesn't hurry." Then, turning to me, she said in a loud voice: "All the servants treat me like this, you know. With absolutely no respect. They forget that I will be mistress of Pennarth someday." She said the words with a sort of recklessness, her eyes blazing.

"Miranda," I said, interrupting her as she muttered

angrily to herself in the corner to which her pacing had led her, "I think that I would rather wait in the hall downstairs. When Mr. Randolph is ready to see me, he can let me know. I hope that you won't be hurt, but——"

"I *will* be hurt!" Her voice seemed to bounce off the book-lined walls, the words beating at one another in mid-air. "I should have known that you would treat me like everyone else. Paul was afraid you liked me. That's why he told me I couldn't go down to your cottage again, but I was going to go. I meant to come and see you tomorrow night, but now I can see you don't want me around. Sometimes I think I might as well kill myself and be dead, like the girl."

"What girl?"

The question slipped out before I had time to think rationally. I knew that I must not involve myself in any kind of intimate discussion with this woman. Particularly not now, and in this place.

"Paul's sister," Miranda said, coming toward me. Her head was lowered so that her dark hair hung about her haggard face, but her eyes were fixed on me. "Eileen. They killed her, you know. Between the two of them they killed her!"

I must have heard the sound of a door opening while she was speaking, but perhaps because of what she had said, it did not register immediately. But now we both turned and saw in the open doorway a man seated in a wheelchair, his hands clutching the wheels, his long white face impassive. He did not say a word, yet there was something terrible about his silence. Uttering a cry, Miranda ran to the door and pushed past him, and I found myself alone with the owner of Pennarth.

Slowly he rolled the wheelchair into the room and reached out to slam the door behind him. Despite the dimness of the light filtering through the mist-shrouded windows, I could see him quite clearly. I had expected a

wizened old man, for I knew he must be in his eighties.
Instead, I found myself staring into clear dark eyes set
deep in a face that could have been that of a skeleton
except for the paper-thin skin that was stretched over the
bones.

The white tunic that he wore dropped from thin shoulders set so flat against the back of the wheelchair that they
might have been nailed to it. His legs were covered with a
plaid rug from which his shoes protruded two narrow
black-leather tips. The wheels of the chair creaked as he
approached me. Only when he was so close to me that his
knees under the rug nearly touched me did he bring himself to a halt.

"It would have been an excellent thing, Miss Grey," he
said in a thin, high-pitched voice, "if you had waited for
an invitation to come to this room."

I should have explained to him that Miranda had
brought me here, but something about this man froze me
into silence. "I'm sorry," I managed to articulate, hating
him as soon as I had spoken for having so quickly managed to put me on the defensive.

"I was told," Mr. Randolph continued stiffly, "that my
daughter-in-law had taken it upon herself to order tea.
Since I eat very little myself, I have remanded the order.
I'm certain you have no desire to gorge yourself alone."

Every word he spoke had the bite of a calculated insult.
I felt myself flush. "I did not come here with the anticipation that it would be a social occasion," I assured him
icily.

"Sit down." It was a command.

"I prefer to stand."

"And I prefer that you sit. It is one of the consequences
of my being confined to this chair that I find it unpleasant
to be looked down on by those who have command of
their legs." The reedy voice rose hysterically. "The sofa is
behind you, Miss Grey. Surely it is not too much to ask
that you lower yourself onto it. Believe me, I do not find it

agreeable to be obliged to appeal to a stranger's sympathies."

I had never been less sympathetic to anyone in my life, but I sat. The skeletal face stretched itself into something resembling a smile.

"It is of considerable interest to me," he said, "to see the young woman who so skillfully managed to ingratiate herself with my sister."

Rage gripped me by the throat. "I came here because I understood that you had something of importance to say to me," I said. "If you prefer to think that I deliberately pandered to your sister, that is your affair. Unless we have something other than my character to discuss, I see no purpose in my remaining here."

"My son is a good judge of character," the old man said reflectively. "You are, I see, more or less what I expected."

I started to rise. I had been angry many times before but never like this. It seemed that unless I was to get away from this man at once, my head would explode.

"Wait!" He stretched out an emaciated arm as though he were about to push me back onto the sofa. "That's right. I do have business to discuss with you, Miss Grey, but I must approach it in my own way. Neither of us desired this interview, but it must be made. If you insist on rushing off hysterically, we will have to meet again. I do not wish to make these arrangements twice. I am not, as you may have guessed, a well man. Even if you manage to remain calm, this meeting will take its toll on my health. I must insist that you remain in this room until I have said what I have to say."

His bony fingers reached for the wheels of his chair, and without any other warning, he turned himself about and rolled himself to the door. It was only when I heard the key turning in the lock that I realized what he had done.

"This is absurd," I heard myself say. "You can't possibly keep me here if I decide to go."

"Ah, but I can, Miss Grey." He wheeled himself about to face me. The key was not in his hand, and I realized that he must have secreted it somewhere on his person. And in that moment anger gave way to fear.

Both of us were silent. The fog was pressed like a gray blanket against the windows, and his face was a thin line of white in the shadows. I thought that he was smiling, but I could not be certain.

"What do you want of me?" I asked, struggling to keep my voice even. I would not, I determined, give him the satisfaction of seeing that I was afraid.

"First, I wish to assure you that I am in complete command of my intellect. That must be understood. You may find it unusual to be locked in a room, but I assure you I have done it simply to assure myself that you will hear me out. All my life, Miss Grey, I have been a man of determined character. Perhaps my sister told you something of that. As long as I had my health it was possible for me to exert my will in a conventional manner. Unfortunately it is now necessary for me to act in—how shall I put it?—a more imaginative fashion at times. I cannot come to you. Therefore you must come here. As you have. And once here, you must meet the terms that I have set for our joint conduct."

He paused, but I did not reply. There seemed to be nothing to say. It would be easy enough to believe that he was mad, but I did not. He meant to have his own way, and I sensed that it would be dangerous to thwart him. Very well. I would listen to what he had to say, and then, presumably, he would unlock the door, and I would leave. I took a deep breath and waited.

"Have you understood what I just said, Miss Grey?" His voice rose shrilly.

"I have."

"Then what is your response?"

"I have none."

"You have nothing to say to me?"

"You asked me here because you had something to say to *me*," I reminded him. "I'm waiting for you to say it."

"And you are in complete control of yourself now?"

I realized that he was trying to bait me. For some reason he wanted me to react to him emotionally. I determined to disappoint him. Whatever response he was accustomed to from women, he would not have it from me.

"Yes," I said dryly. "In complete control."

"Am I what you expected?"

"I had no expectations."

He was, I realized, enjoying this rapid repartee. It was as though he were sharpening his mind on it. Probably, I thought ruefully, to deliver some sort of verbal coup de grace. I did not understand the man. Or trust him. But for the moment I was no longer afraid. I was interested only in leaving this house as soon as possible.

"Surely," he said, "my sister told you something about me."

If I were to tell him the truth, I would have to admit that she had told me nothing. But I knew that I needed to arm myself against this old man, and so I said nothing.

"Probably," he went on, "she told you why she and I quarreled."

"That happened a long time ago," I said. "I don't see that it matters now."

"May I venture to suggest," he said sardonically, "that there are a good many things you do not see, Miss Grey."

He was disembodied by the shadows now. Under any other circumstances the absence of light would have disconcerted me. But at the moment I was just as glad that he could not see my face. I had never lied well, and I knew that my expression would have given me away.

"What happened between you happened a long time ago," I said.

"But you must admit that it is still pertinent."

"Perhaps."

"If you admit that much, you must realize it is impossible that you should stay here."

I chose to deliberately misunderstand him. "I do not intend to stay a moment longer than necessary," I said.

His voice rose, thin and querulous. "I'm talking about your remaining at the cottage," he said. "Don't play the fool, Miss Grey. I'm surrounded by too many of that variety as it is."

"As far as the cottage is concerned," I said, "I intend to remain indefinitely. I'm sure your son informed you of that fact."

The wheels of the chair creaked, and I could see that he was propelling himself slowly toward me. His face was set in bony stiffness, and his shoulders were still pinned against the back of the chair. For the first time it occurred to me that he might not be able to move either his legs or his torso. Obviously he was a very ill man. I had no way of knowing what might happen to him if I seriously angered him. I had a mental image of his toppling forward onto the floor. I clenched my hands together in my lap and found that the palms were wet with perspiration.

"I cannot allow you to stay," he said hoarsely. "You have no legal right to be there."

"Your sister willed me the cottage. As far as her solicitor is concerned, the papers are in order."

"Lawyers!" He spit out the word. "I'm talking about moral right. My father intended that all of Pennarth belong to me ultimately. My sister was left the cottage only for her lifetime. That was what he intended."

"Then he should have arranged matters so that after her death that part of the property would revert to you," I said, breathless with the knowledge that at any moment I might find I had gone too far.

There was a pause. I could hear the old man's shallow breathing in the shadows. It had begun to rain outside, the drops spattering against the window.

"Paul said you intended to drive a hard bargain."

"I assure you, Mr. Randolph, that I did not come here to bargain."

"Five thousand pounds. I'll offer you five thousand pounds. But not a shilling more. That's twice what the place is worth, and you must know it."

"I have no intention of selling the cottage," I said in a low voice. "I told your son that. He preferred to think I was saying that in an attempt to raise the price. He used the word blackmail. . . ."

"It *is* blackmail!"

"No." I rose. "I do not intend to sell the cottage for any price. I'm sorry if it disturbs you so much that I should own it. I told your son that I did not intend to impose my presence on you in any way, and that is true. It's a large estate. There should be no need for you to set eyes on me again or I on you. And now, if you will unlock the door——"

The old man threw back his head suddenly and uttered a sound that could have been a scream of rage. As he toppled against the side of the chair, a key sounded in the lock, and the door was flung open. Paul Randolph appeared, silhouetted by the lights in the corridor behind him. He bent over his father and pulled him upright, pressing his thin shoulders flat against the back of the wheel-chair. The old man's eyes were closed, and he was making curious moaning sounds.

"Get out," Paul Randolph said, raising his head to stare at me. "Get out of here before you succeed in killing him."

I was halfway down the stairs when I met Enoch Lessing, his white head bowed against the effort of the climb. He spoke my name before his eyes had traveled all the way up to my face.

"What's happened, girl?" he puffed, his cherub's face tilted up to mine.

Before I could answer, the strangled sounds that I had

prayed I had left behind reached us. To my bewilderment the old man below me smiled.

"So you've sent him into one of his temper tantrums, have you?" he said. "Now, you know, I thought that might happen if he insisted on seeing you. He's a stubborn man, the elder Mr. Randolph, and he's not used to a bit of defiance now and then. Don't you fret, girl. It will do him good in the end."

"Good!" I exclaimed, glancing back over my shoulder. "He sounds as if he's dying."

"More's the pity that he isn't," Enoch told me. "But it's only his little game to put the fear of God in everyone. Now, don't you look at me like that. I know what I'm saying. There's only one thing we ought to establish. You didn't leave him alone, did you?"

"His son——"

"Ah, that's all right then. I reckoned that young Paul wouldn't be too far away. Keeps a proper eye on his father, he does."

"He told me to leave," I said.

"Can't think you'd want to stay with anything like that going on," Enoch murmured, clutching at the banister as he laboriously turned himself around. "But we can't have you walking back through the rain, can we?"

"I'll be all right," I said, following him in his slow progress down the stairs. The effect of the scene I had just witnessed made me almost as unsteady as the old man in front of me, and I found myself clutching the railing in imitation of him.

"Now, you'll just come along with me," Enoch muttered as we reached the foot of the stairs, where the great hall, sunk in dusk, loomed in front of us. "You just come with me, and no one'll know whether you've left the house or not."

I started to protest, but he put his hand on my arm and led me slowly to a green-baize-covered door set in an alcove. Beyond the door was a narrow corridor illuminated by a single bare light bulb. The worn linoleum beneath our feet gave testimony to the fact that we were now in the servants' quarters. Somewhere at the rear of the hall I could hear the clatter of dishes.

"My room's just here," Enoch said heavily, pushing open a door to our right. He stood aside to let me pass in front of him. "That's right. In you go. We'll have a cup of tea and a chat, and likely as not the rain will have let up a bit, and you can go along out the back way and no one the wiser."

I stood in the center of the tiny room and looked about me. This was another world from the ghostly vastness of the main part of the house. Here the ceiling was low and woven with cracks. The wallpaper was redolent with pink cabbage roses, and the two easy chairs drawn up before a coal fire burning in a small black-tiled fireplace were covered with shabby chintz. A chessboard was set out on a low table in front of the fire, and beside it a pipe rested, filled with ashes. There were two windows curtained with the same red material I had found in my cottage. Rain snapped against the panes, but it was clear that it would be difficult for anything to mitigate the coziness of this room.

"This is *your* sitting room?" I asked.

"Does that surprise you, my dear?" The old man grinned at me impishly. "Ah, now I see. You're surprised to find me located here at the back of the house. Do you know, it struck me when I left you this morning that I never had explained my position in relation to this household—if household you can call it. Madhouse is more properly the word. Lena always called it that. Many's the evening she spent here with me just to get away from all of them. That was when we were young, you understand, and her parents were still alive. Cut out of the same piece of cloth as the present master her father was, you understand. And old Mrs. Randolph was a bit odd in her own way."

He was muddling the story, just as he had muddled

everything that he had told me this morning, but it did not seem to matter more now than it had then. The quiet homeliness of the room soothed me, and I sank down onto one of the overstuffed chairs and smiled my relief at him.

"You see, my dear," Enoch continued, brushing his mop of white hair out of his eyes with one gnarled hand, "I'm the elder Mr. Randolph's valet and have been since he came of age and I was a young lad down from London." He chuckled. "I think," he said, "if the truth be known, you took me for a gentleman."

He was right, although I would never have put it in just that way. He was still wearing the well-cut tweed suit he had worn this morning, and although he spoke in a colloquial fashion, his accents could have descended straight from Oxford.

"Oh, I learned their ways," he mused. "There was the uniform until a few years ago, of course, and a uniform does mark a man. But I'm retired now, in a manner of speaking, and my clothes are my own affair. Still I expect I couldn't fool anyone for long. That was what I used to tell Lena. 'You can make a sow's ear look like a silk purse, my dear,' I'd say, 'but you can't turn it into the genuine article.' But that's no matter now. The thing we want at present is our tea. I'll just tell one of the girls we'll be needing another cup and some of that seedcake I smelled baking this morning."

He shuffled out the door, leaving me alone. The realization that for fifty years or more this delightful old man had been the manservant of the spectral invalid I had just met was bewildering, simply because it made more confusing his relationship to Lena Randolph. What was it Enoch had said? That he had become her brother's valet at the time her brother had come of age.

Miss Randolph was eighty-two when she died. Her brother was, I knew, only a few years older. That would mean she must have been about eighteen when Enoch had come to Pennarth. I wondered if he had been handsome. It would have been natural that the two had been attracted to one another: natural if one did not take into account the considerable social barriers that would have stood automatically in their way in England at the beginning of the century.

If they had met, if she had come to this room to escape her family, it must have been done secretly. She had told me once that her father had died when she was in her early twenties and her mother five years later. Did that mean that for nearly a decade she had managed to conduct a secret romance with a man there could have been little chance of her marrying? She had said that she had remained at Pennarth after it became her brother's property because of her mother. But had it, in fact, been Enoch who had kept her here—Enoch who had been the real tie? Had she once dreamed of the day when, as the inheritor of part of some of her father's capital, she and her brother's valet could have escaped?

Perhaps it was the blue flames of the tiny coal fire that made me want to close my eyes and think of nothing except the tea Enoch had promised me. What had happened so long ago, even what was happening now in the other part of the house, did not really concern me. I had promised myself that I would not become involved in these people's lives. And yet. . . .

My eyes fell on a portrait of a young woman in a gilt-edged frame on a table across the room. Even at this distance there was something familiar about the features. Conscious that I was prying and yet not able to resist, I rose and went to examine it and found myself looking into Miss Randolph's eyes. The picture must have been taken when she was very young. Her face was soft and unlined, and her hair was dark and caught in a coil at the top of her head. Despite her youth and the old-fashioned gown, snugged tight about a tiny waist, she was completely recognizable as the old woman I had nursed for three years.

Suddenly the tragedy of her life struck me with full

force. She must have loved Enoch very much to have corresponded with him daily for so many years. I remembered those thin, wrinkled fingers dispatching letter after letter into the flames and felt tears burn my eyes. Why had Enoch not followed her when she had left Pennarth? She had had the courage to tear herself away. Why had he not gone with her? She had come back from time to time to stay in seclusion at the cottage. They must have met there. What force had kept them from making a life together?

In my mind's eye I abruptly saw the face of her brother, the white lifeless skin stretched across the bones of his face, the shoulders set rigidly against the back of the wheelchair. Had it been because of him that one woman had spent her life separated from the man she loved, that another had been driven to suicide, and that still another woman was kept a literal captive in this house? Had he been able to ruin the life of one woman after another on the sharp edge of fear?

The opening of the sitting-room door brought me back to reality. With an agility I had not suspected, Enoch came into the room bearing a tray on which were set teapot, cups, and a plate piled generously with cake. I went to take the burden from him. Muttering his thanks, he closed the door carefully behind him, slid the bolt in place, and shuffled to the fireplace to clear the low table of the chess set so that I could set the tray there.

"Generally, you understand," he said, puffing his way into a chair, "Martha brings me tea at five, but the little crisis upstairs has set the girls in the kitchen chattering like a group of sparrows, and they were quite happy to have me help myself. I thought it was better not to advertise the fact that I was entertaining company. It will be much better for all concerned if you are thought to have left the house."

I hesitated beside the other chair. "Perhaps I ought to go," I said. "I wouldn't want you to get into any trouble because of me."

"No, no. Sit down, my dear. It isn't often that I have the opportunity to entertain an attractive young lady for tea. And, I assure you, we will not be disturbed. In the old days, of course, I would have been called immediately to the elder Mr. Randolph's side. Lately, however, he would rather have his son near him. It's only natural, considering the nature of his illness, that he should want someone with the strength to move him about. No, I assure you, Miss Grey, my position now is one of pensioner."

I was no more able to refuse him now than I had been this morning. I sat down opposite him and poured the tea while he sat watching me contentedly, his hands folded over the hillock of his stomach.

"Ah, it takes one back," he said as I bent across the table to place the cup and saucer in his hands. "A man's a fool to deprive himself of the company of women. Mind you, I don't include the kitchen staff and the maids in that category, although women they are technically. But the maids—village girls, you know—they come, and they go. And the cook is a demon who saves her sweet words for the stew. Anyway she gave notice today and left, bag and baggage—something Miranda did, no doubt. And Martha. She's not to be trusted."

I remembered the hard-faced woman who had met me at the door. It had been she whom Miranda had told to serve tea in the library. Instead, she must have reported the request to Mr. Randolph who had rescinded it.

The tea was fresh and hot. As I drank it I felt my self-possession return. "Precisely what is wrong with Mr. Randolph?" I asked the cherubic old man across the table from me.

"Paralysis, my dear. He suffered a stroke two years ago, and that did the damage. For myself, I am putting my trust in my heart. Or rather, I trust that when the time comes, it will fail me. It seems a bit much to me that death should humiliate first and then strike down. Mr. Randolph, now, is a pitiful relic of what he once was. His mind grinds as fine as ever, you see, but he must stoop to children's tricks to get his way in small matters. In affairs of importance, as far as members of the family are concerned, of course, he holds the trump cards."

"I'm afraid I don't understand."

"He is the owner of Pennarth, is he not?" Enoch said simply, extending his cup to be refilled with a hand that quavered only slightly. "The house is his, and the grounds. And a substantial fortune as well. Those of us who depend on him for our livelihood are not likely to thwart him when he sets his mind to a particular outcome of events. Of course, you are quite a different matter. He finds himself unable to exert control—and to control has been his life. He cannot cut you from his will. The cottage is, from what I have overheard, quite legally yours. It would perhaps be better if he had before him a possible successful appeal to the law."

"Why better?" I demanded. "Do you want me to be forced to leave?"

"On the contrary, my dear!" The old man's face was rosy from the combined effects of the tea and the fire. "It gives me more pleasure than you will ever know to see that Lena foiled her brother to the end and beyond, if you follow me."

"But surely," I protested, "she didn't leave the cottage to me simply to irritate him."

"Of course not. Lena was, as I am sure you know, incapable of that sort of pettiness. I only meant that if there were a chance that he could dislodge you legally, he would bend all his efforts toward that end. There would be a coming and going of lawyers, and this would keep him pacified. As it is——"

"Yes?"

"As it is, the situation becomes more complex. The elder Mr. Randolph is not a man to give up easily. To be frank, my dear, I do not like to think of you down there alone."

I stared at him. "You're certainly not suggesting," I said in a low voice, "that he would——"

"He is capable of anything." The pink face dissolved in a mass of creases as the old man frowned. "Believe me, I would not try to frighten you unnecessarily, but you must be on your guard. And to be on one's guard is frequently a disturbing experience. Much as I like to see the cottage lived in again, I think you ought to reconsider your decision to remain there."

Despite the fact that I was certain he was exaggerating, a tingle of fear slid up my backbone. "You aren't suggesting that anything would happen to me if I stayed, are you?" I said, smiling and taking a seedcake.

I was not hungry, but suddenly it had become imperative that I appear self-assured. I instinctively trusted Enoch, but my instinct had played me false in the part. Whatever the ties keeping him at Pennarth for all these years, they must be strong. And as he himself had pointed out, he was a dependent of Mr. Randolph's. The owner of this estate had tried with veiled threats to force me to leave. Surely it was conceivable that the man who had been his servant for over a half century might have been told to frighten me away if he could.

Enoch's pale-blue eyes did not leave my face. "Life could be made unpleasant for you," he said slowly.

"But how?" I insisted. "I assure you I will never come here again. I intend to lead my own life. Quietly. You've already said that Mr. Randolph won't be able to create legal difficulties. What other kind of harassment could there be?"

The old man heaved his rotund body forward and set his empty cup on the table. "Ah, my dear," he said, "you are a determined woman. You make me think of——"

"Of Lena?" I suggested when he paused, his eyes fixed absently on the wall behind me.

"No, not of Lena. When she was as young as you, she was still malleable. Her strength of character came later.

But once there was another girl, a girl who thought she could have her way with him."

"Are you talking about his daughter?" I said in a low voice. "Are you talking about Eileen?"

Enoch's twisted fingers caught and gripped the edge of the table. "Eileen?" he exclaimed. "What do you know about her? I warn you, my dear girl, it would be unwise—"

He broke off, his eyes darting toward the door. I turned and saw that the knob was being turned slowly from the outside. And then the knock sounded. Puffing, Enoch pushed himself out of his chair and started across the room, giving me a bewildered look.

"No one ever disturbs me," he muttered, brushing his white hair back from his eyes. "No one."

"It's all right," I assured him. "After all, we haven't committed a crime. At all events, I was just about to leave."

I followed him to the door and waited while his uncertain fingers fumbled with the bolt. I remembered how Miranda had told me that when her father-in-law came to the library, she would hide from him. I had thought it an odd thing for her to suggest at the time, but now I sympathized with the impulse. There was something about this house that encouraged hiding. But I refused to succumb. I had been told to leave the house, and I was leaving it now. It was that simple—at least it seemed to be until the door swung open, and I found myself facing Paul Randolph.

For a moment no one spoke. Paul's face was very pale, and I was suddenly reminded of his father. There was the same static quality about him, the same stiffness—a sort of immobility. His dark eyes fastened on mine. He stared at me expressionlessly.

"We meet again, Miss Grey," he said.

It was a rebuke and at the same time, a deliberate insult.

"It was at my insistence that the young lady stayed," Enoch said with a false buoyancy that would have fooled no one. "The rain——"

"I'm about to leave," I said. I turned to the old man beside me and extended my hand. "I enjoyed the tea," I said. "Thank you."

Enoch gripped my hand in both of his. His pink face seemed to quiver as though he were about to burst into tears. "My dear girl," he said, "are you certain that you can find your way in this fog? Perhaps you would allow me to accompany you."

"I will take care of that part of it," Paul said in a hard voice. "I can drive her back."

"I prefer to walk," I said.

"Then I will walk with you." His voice was decisive. "If you will follow me, I will provide you with a raincoat."

Turning on his heel, he started off down the corridor in the direction of the main part of the house. I loosened my hand from Enoch's grasp.

"I prefer to go alone," I said.

Paul Randolph came to a halt. He did not turn. "I'm quite sure that you do," he said, "and I can assure you that if it were not for the fog, I would let you do so. As it is you would undoubtedly lose your way. Now if you will come with me. . . ."

His hand was on the green-baize door. "Go with him," I heard Enoch mutter.

I shrugged my shoulders. Obviously there was nothing else I could do. I walked out into the hallway and turning to smile my assurance at the old man, detected a furtive movement in the doorway that I guessed led to the kitchen. Enoch saw it, too. His mouth framed the name Martha. I nodded, understanding what he meant to tell me.

He had been right when he suggested that the house-keeper was not to be trusted. He had not taken the extra cup from the kitchen unnoticed, as he had thought, and she had gone to Paul to tell him that I was still in the house.

Paul held the door open for me, and I passed him without turning my head. The great hall loomed in front of me like a shadowy cavern. There was no sound except that of our steps across the vast room. By the arched door Paul paused and opened a closet, the door of which was indistinguishable from the paneled wall. In silence he held out a coat to me and took one for himself. The enveloping folds of the garment told me that it must be Miranda's, and I remembered the incongruous sight she had presented in my orange dressing gown. I waited while Paul opened the door, and together we went out into a fog so thick that I could not see the steps in front of me.

I let him take my arm. There was no help for it. I knew he did not want to touch me any more than I wanted him to. But the impenetrable mist rising from an unseen sea had bound us together for a short moment in time. I felt the gravel under my shoes and knew that we had reached the drive. The sound of our steps rose, muffled, strangely muted as though we were encased in a soft gray cylinder. The rain seemed to have stopped, or perhaps the mist had absorbed that, too. Moisture masked my face, and I could feel my hair grow heavy with it.

"It's often like this," I heard Paul say. His voice seemed to come to me down a hollow funnel from a great distance.

The fog was so thick that although I could still feel his hand on my arm, I could see only the misted outlines of him, the collar of his raincoat turned high about his face as it had been the night he had come to the cottage after Miranda. It was strange, I realized suddenly, that I never thought of her as his wife, but rather as his captive—as I was his captive now.

"People talk about the beauty of Cornwall," he continued, as though he were talking to himself, "but they forget the weather. They come here in the summer, and they pack the beaches and muck around with their boats and talk about how wonderful it is. But they don't see much of this sort of thing, and it's what we put up with three seasons out of four. Fog and a lot of rain. And the cold in the winter. It's a particular kind of damp, penetrating cold you have to experience to appreciate."

This was, I supposed, just another gambit to convince me that I was a fool to think of living the year round at the cottage. And I was becoming unutterably weary of it: weary of his father and his threats, weary of the black negativism that I seemed to encounter with everyone, even Enoch. "I'm surprised," I said, "that if it's as unpleasant as you say, you remain here."

He made no response to that. I had meant to annoy him. "I hope," I said, "that your father is all right."

"Do you?"

It was a fair comment. He must know that I had no interest in the old man's well-being or lack of it. I had been rebuked, and perhaps I deserved it. I was surprised when he spoke again without any particular enmity in his voice.

"My father is a very strong man," he said. "Considering his age and the state of his health, he has remarkable enduring qualities. I'd be interested to know what you said to him to produce that particular reaction, however."

I wanted to suggest that since he had apparently been waiting outside the door, he might very well know precisely what I had said, but at the same time I knew that would be unnecessary viciousness on my part.

"Didn't he talk to you about it?" I asked.

"Obviously he did not, or I wouldn't have asked you," Paul snapped. "He was too upset to be coherent. And he is a man who prefers to keep his own counsel."

"Obviously he told you that he intended to make an offer for the cottage," I said, "since you mentioned it to me yesterday."

"And the offer has been made?"

"Made and rejected. It's unfortunate that you didn't convey that information to him yesterday. It would have saved everyone a great deal of trouble."

I had, it seemed, successfully terminated another conversation. We walked in silence at a snail's pace. Even Paul seemed to walk into the blanket of fog as though he were not certain that the next moment there would be ground under his feet. And yet I knew that we could be nowhere near the cliffs. The mist blanketed sound, true, but there was not even the faintest rumble of the waves. The sensation was very much like that of walking in pitch-darkness with no landmarks to guide your hands. Only the crunch of the gravel under our feet told me that we were still on the drive. It seemed to curve slowly downward, although I could not remember the grade being this steep when I had made my way up to the house.

"We'll turn here," Paul said suddenly. "There's a path that leads diagonally across to the cottage."

I decided that I did not want to leave the main way. I saw the shadow of him turn to the left, but I did not follow. "Wouldn't it be better to stay on the drive?" I said. "Besides, I don't see how you can be certain——"

"I know every inch of this land by heart," he told me, his voice sharp with impatience. "Besides, there's a stone marker here. If you don't believe me, put out your hand."

I did as he told me and felt the wet rough texture of what seemed to be a granite post of some sort. "What is it?" I asked him.

"It's a line boundary." His voice cut through the fog like a knife.

"But aren't we still on the estate?"

I knew that we had to be, but that nagging sense of panic returned. If only I could see something in the whirling whiteness around me. I could not even seen Paul now. He was not far away, but for a moment I sensed what it would be like to be alone in this blind world and realized that if he had decided we would take the path, I would have to go with him. But still I delayed.

"These are the boundary markers for the land that goes with the cottage," he said. "There's another here by me. I'm surprised that you haven't traced them already. My aunt had them erected as a reminder to my father as to where his property ended and hers began."

"But I thought . . ." I began and then let my voice trail off into a hollow silence. Why should I tell him I had believed that the land I had inherited was restricted to the plot of grass surrounding the cottage itself?

"How far is it to my—to the house?" I asked him.

"Only a few minutes' walk." He moved back toward me, and I could see the dark outline of him facing me. "I take it," he said in a thoughtful voice, "that you didn't realize any land was attached to the cottage rights. You're a rather contradictory person, Miss Grey. On the one hand, you are determined to hang on to your inheritance, yet you haven't even bothered to check the extent of your rights. Perhaps this will make it clearer to you why my father is so upset. He's an old man, Miss Grey, and this estate has been his life. I could count the times he's left it since he was a boy at school on the fingers of one hand. You ought to consider sometime what a blow it was to him to have a three-acre section carved out of it, subdivided as though it were some sort of housing estate."

"That was his father's decision," I said defensively.

"My grandfather was a very sick man when he made his last will," Paul said. "It was not too difficult, from what I hear, for him to be what an attorney might call unduly influenced."

"By whom?"

"By his wife. My aunt was always my grandmother's favorite. I realize you've probably been told a lot of nonsense about my father's character, but——"

"I was told nothing," I protested. "Whatever you may think, your aunt was not a malicious person. I understood that there had been some quarrel between her and your father, but she never discussed the details of it. And she certainly never maligned him."

"So you understood that there had been a quarrel, did you?" Paul's laugh was unpleasant. I was glad in that moment that I could not see his face. "Come now, Miss Grey," he said. "Don't you think all this innocence is a bit absurd at this point?"

"Contrary to what you seem to believe," I snapped, "I know very little about your family affairs, and unintelligible as it may seem to you, I don't want to know any more. Now, Mr. Randolph, if you want to lead the way. . . ."

I started toward him, but he did not turn. For a moment we were so close that even through the mist I could see his face clearly, the high cheekbones glistening with moisture, those strange dark eyes so like his father's. I stepped aside, determined to walk around him if I had to, and found myself engulfed in wet shrubbery and felt his hand on my arm, this time gripping it tightly.

"What do you expect me to believe," he said in a low voice, "when not more than fifteen minutes ago I heard you talking with Enoch about my sister?"

I tried to pull away from him, but his fingers were like a restraining band.

"I don't know what you're talking about," I muttered. "Let go of me."

"I'm talking about Eileen. You've made it a point to find out about Eileen, haven't you?"

"I didn't 'find out' anything," I said. "I was told—"

I pressed my lips tight shut, knowing that I had said more than I had meant to say.

"Who told you? I can believe that my aunt gave you a considerable amount of information. I do believe that, no matter what you say. But she never knew Eileen. She left this place long before my sister was born. Even when Eileen died—"

Now it was his time to curb himself. His hand loosened

on my arm, and I shook it away and stepped back into the safety of the mist.

"Was it Enoch?" I heard him say. "He's an old fool in a good many ways, but I would never have thought he would talk to anyone outside the family about her."

Already poor Enoch probably faced the blame of having invited me to his sitting room when I should have left the house. I did not intend that he be faulted for anything else because of me.

"No," I said. "The only reason Mr. Lessing mentioned her name was because I spoke of her first."

"Then how——"

"Ron Farrow told me," I said. "I happened to meet him at my friends' house when I went in to St. Ives the other day. When he learned that I was living here at Pennarth, he told me about her." As soon as I had mentioned Ron's name, I felt a sense of betrayal, as though I had betrayed a trust. I did not want to discuss the confidences of someone like Ron—someone I had felt so drawn to—with this dark, angry man.

It was so long before Paul Randolph made any response that I began to think he had left me alone to get back to the cottage any way I could. We had the ability to infuriate one another almost instantly. I promised myself that I would go to a great deal of trouble in the future to avoid exchanging any words with him. But then, that was what I had told myself the day before, after he had driven me back from St. Ives. Now, not more than twenty-four hours later, I was involved in another verbal altercation with him. Even though the prospect of trying to get back to the cottage through this impenetrable fog daunted me, I found myself hoping that he had left me. And then he spoke.

"Ron Farrow," he muttered. "I thought he was in London."

Perhaps it was my imagination, but I thought there was menace in his voice. I dreaded the moment when he might reach out again through the mist and take my arm. I did not know what sort of man he was. It was quite possible that he had good reason to hate Ron. I was probably being absurdly melodramatic, but it occurred to me that he might try to force me to tell him more about Ron. Once he knew that Ron was staying at St. Ives, he might seek him out.

There was too much I did not understand. I knew only that I could not stay here with him. He had said that it was only a few minutes down this path to the cottage. Without giving myself time to think, I pushed past him and started to run, my outstretched hands brushing the bushes on both sides of me. I could feel the hard-packed earth of the path under my feet. It seemed to run straight. Perhaps it would be easier than I had anticipated to make my escape.

I heard him calling my name, and his voice seemed to come from a great distance. I stumbled over a root and fell heavily against the trunk of a tree, rubbing the palms of my hands raw against the rough bark.

"Sara!"

Formalities were forgotten now, I noted grimly, beginning to run again. The fog seemed to be suffocating me. I was breathless. But I was still on the path—I had not lost it—and in a minute the cottage would unfold itself in front of me, and this absurd nightmare would be over.

The ground bent upward now, and the trees and bushes seemed to have fallen away from me. I guessed that I must be in the clearing where the cottage was set. I slackened my pace but not in time to avoid the rock face that suddenly loomed up in front of me. I fell against it and lay there, stunned, letting the thick silence settle over me.

Then, as I tried to get to my feet, I heard the sound of running feet behind me. Clawing at the rock face, I pulled myself erect and felt a sharp, searing pain in my right ankle. Involuntarily I cried out.

"For God's sake, don't move! Stay where you are!"

He was close behind me now. I tried to take a step and

cried out again. Then his hands were on me, and he was turning me about, holding me close against him.

"You fool!" he muttered. "You little fool! Don't you know where you are? A few more steps, and you would have been over the side of the cliff."

4

"But I couldn't hear the sea. I couldn't hear the sea."

I repeated the words over and over again as Paul led me down the slope, half supporting me. My ankle pained me, but I scarcely noticed. I knew he was right, that somehow I had managed to pass the cottage and climb the slope that led to the promontory.

I could not let myself believe that if I had taken a few steps more, there would suddenly have been nothing beneath my feet but empty air. In my imagination I experienced the sensation of falling, as one does in a dream. I began to shiver and could not stop.

"It's all right," Paul said in a low voice. "It's all right."

I closed my eyes against the mist. "I couldn't hear the sea," I said again.

"Sound doesn't carry when the fog is this thick," he told me. His voice was gentle. "Don't think about it. We're at the cottage now. I'm going to carry you up the steps. I don't want you to put any weight on that foot."

It was obvious that he was perfectly familiar with the cottage. He mounted the two stone steps with no hesitation and swinging the door open, lowered me to the floor and flicked the wall switch.

"You shouldn't leave the place unlocked," he said, supporting me with one hand while he closed the door with the other. "Now, we'll get you to a chair and look at that ankle."

Even the scant light shed by the rose-shaded lamp in the corner by the fireplace blinded me. I rubbed my eyes as he lowered me into one of the easy chairs and looked around, feeling relief rise inside me. I had been a fool to think that this man kneeling on the floor in front of me, touching my ankle with gentle fingers, could have wanted to harm me. He might have been angry, but I had been an idiot to run from him. It must have been the fog that had made me panic, that horrible blinding whiteness that had nearly succeeded in killing me. Even now, safe inside these four walls, I was trembling.

"It's a sprain," Paul said. "Not serious. But it's beginning to swell. Have you got something I can use for a bandage? It needs to be wrapped tightly."

There were rags in the boxroom. In a few minutes he had bathed my ankle in cold water and bound it with an efficiency a doctor might have envied. He helped me out of my raincoat without making it necessary for me to stand and pulled a footstool under my foot. He had probably learned this gentleness, this economy of movement, in taking care of his father. I remembered how quickly he had righted the old man in his wheelchair and suddenly felt ashamed. I could have been more patient with a man so obviously tyrannized by illness. I could have acted with more self-control when Paul himself had pressed me as to what I knew about his sister.

"I'm sorry," I said in a low voice. "I'm sorry that I——"

"It doesn't matter." He stood in front of me, still wearing his raincoat, his dark hair tangled damply on his forehead. "I'm the one who ought to apologize. Look here, you're white as a ghost. Have you got anything to drink?"

"There's brandy in the cupboard by the sink," I said and smiled. It was as much a relief to smile as it had been to escape the fog. "I'll have a glass if you'll take off your coat and join me."

For a moment he hesitated. Then, nodding, as though he had been conducting some sort of inner dialogue, he slipped out of the raincoat, hung it on the rack beside the door, and went into the kitchen.

The brandy steadied me. Perhaps it helped to complete the change in our reaction to one another, too, because there was a new ease in our conversation. For the first time his hostility toward me seemed to have been entirely put down. He let himself sprawl in the other armchair, propping his feet on the fender of the fireplace. For a while neither of us spoke. He was the first to break the silence.

"Do you feel up to talking seriously," he said, his dark eyes moving slowly over my face. "No, don't look like that. I'm not going to try to convince you to leave this place. That part of it is over as far as I'm concerned. But I want to try to explain my position."

"You don't have to," I said in a low voice. "Not unless you want to. I think I understand. But you have to realize one thing. I really meant it when I said I knew nothing about the situation here when I came. I—I had no intention of causing anyone any trouble. I simply wanted to have a chance to paint. No, I don't mean that as any sort of rebuke. I realize now that I've been some sort of catalyst. You don't know anything about me. It's understandable that you might have suspected my motives in coming here. But it's really as simple as this. I have very little money. If I had stayed in London, I would have had to take a job." I shrugged. "Probably it's not necessary for me to tell you all this, but perhaps if in the beginning I'd been more open——"

"I didn't give you much chance, did I?"

Remembering how he had left the cottage with his wife without even saying good-bye, I shook my head.

"Perhaps it would help," he said slowly, "if you understood about Miranda—about my wife. Contrary to what you probably think, it's primarily because of her that I consented to return from London ten years ago. I was a barrister there. It was the sort of life I'd always wanted. People. Excitement. Concerts. Museums. A civilized life. But I gave it all up and came back here."

As though it were something he could not help, the defensiveness was beginning to creep back into his voice again. I had no desire for us to be at one another's throats again. I sensed now that we could be friends and found to my surprise that that was what I wanted. I had always liked the company of men better than women. Bertha had been the only woman with whom I had ever been close. Yet men whose minds I could respect had always seemed to be a rare commodity. And I found this man interesting. It was, I decided, worth being conciliatory, although, perhaps because of my temper, that had always been an attitude I found difficult to cultivate.

"If we're going to talk," I said in a low voice, "you're going to have to take my word for what I think or don't think. Believe me, I never made any judgment about why you might have chosen to stay here."

"But surely it must have occurred to you to wonder why I'd chosen to bury myself in the wilds of Cornwall."

I decided to be honest. We would never get anywhere unless I was. "Yes," I said. "I wondered."

He straightened himself in the chair and leaned toward me, his eyes intense. "And it didn't seem obvious to you that the only reason I might remain is that my father would keep Pennarth from ever coming into my hands unless I did?"

"Is that why?"

My glass was empty. He filled it and then his own. "I

don't know," he said quietly, staring past me. "I won't pretend that he didn't threaten to disinherit me if I didn't come back here to stay, because he did. But I've told myself all these years that I really gave up my own career for a variety of other reasons."

"Such as?"

"Such as the fact that after he had his first stroke, it was necessary for someone to run the estate. It's not just a simple matter of the house and grounds, although there's a great deal of repair that needs to be done." He shrugged. "We had to close up the tower nine years ago. The windows of the north wing were bricked up by my grandfather. Money was running short, even then. There were some valuable paintings in that part of the house. Furniture. He sold the lot. God knows why he felt he had to brick the windows up as well.

"It's a monstrous place now. Great empty rooms. Dead. I suppose the real reason I've stayed here is to try to keep the rest of the house from dying as well. At least that's what I tell myself. For some reason keeping Pennarth alive means a good deal to me." He laughed shortly. "That's probably an inherited weakness. No doubt in another thirty years I'll be the same sort of obsessed, compulsive old man that my father is today."

"No," I said quietly. "I don't think so."

For the first time since I had met him he smiled. It changed his face. It seemed incredible that I could ever have found him remote, hostile, ominous. I knew that he might be deceiving me. And I myself. But somehow it no longer seemed to matter. One thing was obvious. He needed to talk. Perhaps he was pretending to himself that he felt obligated to explain the situation to me. But I guessed that it had been a long time since he had talked to anyone so openly.

"You have more confidence in me than I have in myself," he said. "Or perhaps you're simply being polite. Probably you wish that I stop this—this yattering—and go back to the house."

"No," I said. "Don't go."

The brandy combined with the relief of being safe and sheltered from the fog had combined to make me feel luxuriously relaxed. If my ankle pained me, I no longer felt it. I realized that I must look a fright. I touched my hair and found it to be nearly dry. Without making too much of a point of doing it, I undid the few strands still held by pins and let it fall about my shoulders. In the same moment I sensed that perhaps Paul was not the only person deceiving himself. I did want him to stay, and there might be more to that than I had considered.

Paul was still smiling at me. I had never imagined that his eyes could be so gentle. "Are you sure you're not tired?" he inquired. "Is your ankle uncomfortable?"

I shook my head. "Go on," I said. "Tell me more about why you've stayed here."

"Well." His glass was empty again. He looked reflectively at it and then at the bottle beside him on the table, then leaned back in his chair. "Primarily I think it's a matter of trying to keep the estate a running concern. I started to tell you about that. You see, my father owns three of the clay mines close to here. Tin used to be the big business in Cornwall, but foreign competition took care of that a long time ago. But clay is still the thing.

"There's a manager, of course, but my father always made the important decisions, and since he hasn't been able to involve himself actively, well, that's been my affair. Not that he still doesn't involve himself. He'd die if he wasn't involved. But he depends on me to keep him informed. He claims I'm the only person he trusts, and that only because he says I'm the person who will profit from it. Unfortunately it's his theory that the only people who take any real interest in a business are the people who stand to make the greatest immediate gains."

I leaned back my head and laughed. For some strange reason it had been a long time since I had felt so happy. "Perhaps," I suggested, "it's true."

"Most cynical philosophies are," Paul admitted. "And the

fact remains that unless those clay mines are kept productive, Pennarth will end up in the hands of strangers."

He was no longer smiling, and I noticed that his hands were clenched about the arms of the chair.

"You'd hate that, wouldn't you?" I murmured.

"Yes. I'd hate that!" Suddenly he rose and went from window to window, pulling the red drapes. "I'm sorry," he said. "I'm on edge. It's that damn fog."

I was glad he had shut us out from it completely, but I knew that it was not spring air thick with moisture that had created the tension in him.

"You said a minute ago," I murmured, "that you wanted to keep the estate intact. It's not really intact, is it, as long as this cottage and the three acres belong to someone else?"

He came to stand in front of me. His eyes held mine. "It never really bothered me as long as it belonged to my aunt," he said slowly. "As far as my father was concerned, to even mention his sister was like waving a red cloth in front of a bull. But there was more to that than this cottage, of course. No, as long as it was hers, it didn't bother me. After all, technically she was part of the family. A Randolph." He laughed bitterly.

"But then I came along," I prompted him.

"Yes." His voice was so low that I could scarcely hear him. "Yes, then you came along, Sara."

He had spoken my name before when he had run after me through the fog, but that was then. And this was now. Somehow it seemed as if I had never really heard my name spoken by anyone before. In that instant I knew that I should tell him to go, but I said nothing. Eons seemed to pass before he wrenched his eyes away from mine.

"No," he said, turning away from me, "it doesn't bother me that this part of Pennarth belongs to you. Can you believe that?"

"Yes. I can believe it."

He was smiling again when he turned back to face me.

Sinking down in his chair again, he glanced at the bottle a second time.

"Another drink?" I said softly.

"No. It's easy enough to talk to you without drinking. But perhaps you're hungry. I don't know whether I interrupted you and Enoch before you had a chance to have your tea."

"Later," I murmured. "Later we'll eat."

"And in the morning I'll take you to the doctor if the swelling in that ankle hasn't gone down."

I nodded. We had set up a continuity, and I knew it. I would see him again tomorrow. And I did not have to look beyond tomorrow to feel utter contentment.

"I said there was another reason why I came here and stayed."

I did not answer him, but the contentment fled as quickly as it had come.

"Miranda," he said. And then was silent.

"She's not well?" my voice was sharper than I had intended it to be, but he did not appear to notice.

"She had what is commonly called a nervous breakdown," he said, "while we were still living in London. No apparent cause other than the fact that there had been no—no children."

He was finding this difficult to say, but I could think of no words to help him. I had never expected to pity him, and I did not pity him now. He was too obviously a man totally capable of handling his own affairs, and it was absurd that I should not want him to tell me about her. No, not "her." His wife. I had welcomed his confidences until this moment. It was no time to let a sense of delicacy creep into the situation.

"Has it helped?" I said. "Her being here?"

He tensed. His face seemed to sharpen, until once again I saw the resemblance to his father clearly. Too clearly. "You've seen her," he said. "Talked to her."

"But I don't know how she was before," I reminded him.

"You knew as soon as you had exchanged two words with her that there was something wrong."

I remembered the gaiety with which she had greeted me when I had found her in the car. "She seems lonely," I said.

"Nothing more than that?"

"No," I said. "She's troubled, obviously. She—she seems to think of herself as some sort of prisoner."

"In a sense she is." His voice was grim. His eyes no longer met mine. "And I'm the jailer. That's what you think, isn't it?"

I smiled my rebuke. "You weren't going to tell me what I think or don't think. Remember? I'm not in any position to be critical. It's a difficult situation. You have to deal with it as you see best."

He laughed bitterly. "You know," he said, "there was a time when there was absolutely no doubt in my mind that I was always right."

"I thought I detected a few remnants of self-assurance," I murmured.

He was sensitive to my moods. He saw at once that he was being teased. Although he did not move, I could sense him relax again.

"You know," he said, "you're a very unusual woman. In an odd way you remind me of my sister." His face darkened. "You know what happened to her, don't you?"

"Yes." I whispered the word.

"Did you know that she was pregnant when she died?" It was clear that he was struggling to keep his voice even. His eyes no longer met mine.

I nodded.

"Then Ron Farrow knew." It was as though he were talking to himself.

"Not until afterward," I told him. "And then only because of the rumors in the village."

"Tell me." He raised his eyes, and I was appalled at the agony I saw in them. "Does he admit that he was the father?"

We were on dangerous ground. I did not want to alienate him again, but I could not lie any more than I could brush the question away.

"He said that they used to meet here," I murmured. "In this cottage."

Paul leaned forward, gripping his hands between his knees. "Do you think I didn't know that?" he demanded. "Do you think that wasn't the reason that she was sent away to school? That's an example of what I meant when I said there was a time when I was certain that every decision I made was the right one. School!" He rose from the chair, his face twisted with bitterness. "I should have killed him—before he succeeded in killing her."

When someone knocked on the door of the cottage at a little after ten that night, I was certain that it must be Paul, although when he had left me three hours before, he had given no indication of intending to return before morning. After his outburst against Ron, he had become quiet, obviously distracted by his own thoughts. He had fixed me a sketchy dinner from odds and ends he found in the refrigerator but had not stayed to share it with me, muttering something about his father expecting him.

Just before he left, he examined the ankle again and told me that since the swelling was already subsiding, there might be no need for me to see a doctor but that he would come down the next morning to make sure. He was friendly enough, but that intimacy I had sensed growing between us had disappeared or had been pushed out of sight. The fog was dispersing when he opened the door to leave. I sat for a long time after he left, staring at the oak panels of the door, feeling, for some odd reason, more alone than I had ever felt before.

Perhaps, because he had left me lonely, I subconsciously hoped that he would return. I know only that I was about to hobble up the stairs to bed when the knock came and that my heart began to beat fast as I awkwardly made my way across the low-ceilinged passageway. When I saw Ron Farrow standing in the doorway, I was disappointed. There's little use in pretending otherwise. And that emotion must have showed in my face, for his smile faded, and he made no attempt to come inside.

"I know it's late," he began.

"That doesn't matter." Belatedly I tried to cover my own rudeness. "Come in."

The night was clear now. Over his shoulder I could see, beyond the trees, the stars spangling the sky. Instead of moving forward, Ron turned away from me and sank down on the stone step, pressing his hands against his forehead. The light from inside the door caught his blond head in a halo of soft light. Leaving the door open, I managed to lower myself down beside him without putting my weight on my left foot. "I shouldn't have come," I heard him mutter.

I suddenly realized that I did not know how to react to him. When he had told the story of himself and Paul's sister, I felt a great wave of sympathy for him and for the frightened girl he had loved. I had hated the forces that had worked against them. And, of course, he had meant me to hate.

Now the very fact that he had been so open with someone who was no more than a stranger to him somehow seemed suspect. I had been ready to believe anything he had told me about Paul and his father then. Now I saw things differently. I remembered the bitterness in Paul's face when he declared that Ron had killed his sister. I told myself at the moment of his outburst that he could not have been speaking of murder. What he must have meant was that since Ron had made her pregnant, he had ultimately been responsible for her suicide. But I had, for a moment, seen Ron through his eyes. Now it was impossible for me to react to Ron dispassionately.

"It's the first time I've been back here since—since Eileen died," Ron said. His hands still shielded his face from my view, but his voice was that of someone struggling with torment. I felt myself softening toward him.

"Why did you come?" I said in a low voice.

"Because I had to." He raised his face from his hands and turned toward me. His eyes glittered angrily in the light pouring out the half-opened door behind us.

"Ever since I talked to you," he went on, "I've known that I had to come back here. I started out this morning, then turned back. But I hated myself for not having the courage to come. I tried to work, but it wasn't any good. Seeing you at Bertha's, knowing that you were living here—it brought it all back.

"I thought I had put it behind me, don't you see? That's why I told you about Eileen. As a sort of test. A test of myself. I'd never talked about it before. I don't care if you believe that or not. But when you said you were living at the cottage, I thought that I could—but I couldn't. It doesn't matter how many years have passed. It's never going to be just a story."

I knew what he was trying to tell me. He had thought that by returning, by actually seeing me living here, he could exorcise a ghost. Now he realized there were some things that could never be overcome.

"Come inside," I suggested. "Perhaps if you can do that——"

"No!" He stared into the night, his face tight.

The stone step was hard and uncomfortable. I started to rise, forgetting my ankle, and cried out as pain shot through my leg.

"What's wrong with your foot?" For the first time since he had come his eyes seemed to focus on me.

"I fell," I said. "It's nothing. Only a simple sprain."

"Fell?" he demanded. "Where?"

"I was walking in the fog," I said, trying to keep my voice light. "There was a stone in my way." I shrugged my shoulders and laughed.

"You're a fool to walk anywhere around here in the fog," Ron said harshly. "At least not until you know your way about better than you do. You're too close to those cliffs."

He broke off, staring at his clenched hands. I realized that he was going through the familiar process of imagining Eileen's fall onto the rocks. Now, ironically enough, I knew even better than he what it must have been like with her that night except that she had not heard Paul's voice calling her name as she ran through the darkness, except that she had known where she was going. The abrupt drop into space could have come as no surprise to her, and as I thought that, I was touched with a sudden chill.

How did I know that my mental image was the true one? How did I know that she was alone on the night she died? That she had cast herself over the precipice with any more deliberation than I would have done had I taken one step more?

I was aware now that Ron was watching me. "Tell me," he said, "how do you like Paul Randolph?"

The question startled me. "I scarcely know the man," I said. "Why? What makes you ask?"

"I saw you drive out of St. Ives with him in that sports car of his yesterday," Ron said. "I thought it was odd. You gave the impression, at Bertha's, that you weren't intending to see much of the family."

I was amazed at the power of my own resentment—resentment that he should have seen Paul and me and, more than that, that he should feel free to ask me any questions about my life. Yet I knew I was being unreasonable. I would not have felt this way yesterday. But now I did not want to talk about Paul with anyone. I wanted to keep my relationship with him—whatever that relationship was—private.

"He happened to see me waiting at the bus stop," I replied, "and he offered to give me a ride back here. There's nothing too unusual about that, is there?"

Ron stared at me curiously. "Why so hostile?" he said in a low voice.

"I'm not hostile," I retorted.

"It's just that you don't think who you see or don't see is any of my business."

"You're making something out of nothing," I told him. Although the fog had lifted, the night air was damp, and I felt chilled—chilled and exhausted.

"Then why is it so important to you that I don't mention Paul Randolph?"

"It's not important," I said, angry now and not bothering to hide the fact. I wanted to get up, go into the cottage, and slam the door behind me. But at the same time I realized that I could not rise from this step unless he helped me.

"I'm very tired," I said.

"I can imagine that you are," Ron said in an insinuating voice. "It must have been a strain seeing old Randolph. Did he manage to beat you down? Are you going to leave?"

"How do you know that I saw him?" The words burst out involuntarily. Once said, it was too late to take them back. I cursed myself for not having phrased my response differently. I could have put it differently and not committed myself. I could have lied.

"Perhaps I guessed," Ron answered. He was smiling a thin, unpleasant smile. "It was obvious to me at least that he wouldn't leave you alone."

"No," I said. "You knew. You weren't guessing."

He shrugged. "Have it your own way," he said. "Are you leaving?"

"No. Now if you'll help me get up——"

"There's no hurry. What did you and the old man talk about?"

"I can't think that would be of any interest to you."

"Can't you? Tell me, did he discuss his daughter? Did he tell you about Eileen?"

"Of course not. What are you getting at?"

"Actually I didn't think he would," Ron said. "Talk about her, that is. But I imagine that Paul wasn't as reticent. Not once he knew that you had talked to me."

I stared at him, bewildered. He had come too near to the truth too many times. Had he been here earlier, lurking about in the mist? Had he followed Paul and me as we made our way down the path from Pennarth? Had he heard Eileen's name? I shook my head. I was letting my imagination run away with me. He had simply made two very accurate guesses, that was all. I had verified the first without thinking, but now I was determined not to tell him anything more.

"Perhaps all this makes sense to you," I snapped, "but it certainly doesn't to me. Help me up. I don't want to talk about this anymore."

"So he's managed to turn you against me already."

I hated that sardonic note in his voice, and my temper flared. "You come here and talk in riddles," I said, "and you expect me to be delighted. There's no possible way that Paul Randolph could have known that I was acquainted with you unless I chose to tell him. And whether I did that or not is my own affair. It can't possibly matter."

I started to push myself into a standing position, determined to ignore the pain, but Ron reached out and roughly pushed me back against the steps. Suddenly I was afraid.

"Didn't it occur to you," he said rapidly, "that it might not have been a coincidence that Paul Randolph happened to meet you in St. Ives? Didn't it occur to you that he might have followed you there, that he might have been watching outside Greg and Bertha's, that he might have seen me go inside? Didn't it occur to you that he might think that you deliberately sought me out?"

I stared at him. "Why would I have done that?" I demanded. "You're being absurd. There wouldn't be any possible reason—"

"Think for a minute, will you?" Ron's voice was tense. "For three years you've been a companion to an old woman who had good reason to hate Pennarth and everyone who lives there. An old woman who knew better than anyone what her brother was capable of. A woman who may have suspected that her niece's death wasn't as simply explained as it had been."

"Miss Randolph didn't even know Eileen," I protested. "She hadn't been back here since she was born. I never had any indication that she even knew the details of how she died."

"Of course she knew the details," Ron said scornfully. "She was in constant touch with Enoch Lessing, wasn't she?"

"I don't know how you could possibly know that." My voice was shrill, ranging out of control.

"How I happen to know anything is beside the point. The fact is that the old woman was aware of everything that went on in that house until the day she died. Do you think anyone believes that she left you this cottage as a gesture of friendship?"

"But she did. She had no other reason——"

"She could have given you a commission," Ron said impatiently. "There could have been something she wanted done, something she couldn't do herself. Her final revenge. A cottage wouldn't have been too great a price for her to pay."

"To pay for what?" I demanded.

"My guess is that she sent you here to find out what really happened to Eileen Randolph. Enoch Lessing must have told her something that made her believe that Eileen's death wasn't an accident. She'd had her own life ruined by her brother, and nearly a half century later she saw another girl, a girl very much like herself——"

"Stop it!" I said. "I've told you before that I don't want to hear any more, and it's true. You've let this—this thing that happened to Eileen obsess you. And now you're hal-

lucinating. I've said this before, and I'll say it again: I had
no other motive for coming here than wanting to be left in
peace in order to paint. You ought to be able to understand that. I don't know anything about what went on here
fifty years ago or twenty years ago or last week, and I
don't want to know. And it won't do you any good to try
to make me tell you anything else, because that's all there
is to it. Now, are you going to let me go inside that house
or not?"

For a moment his blue eyes penetrated mine, then he
took a deep breath and rose to his feet. He put out his
hand, and I took it and let him pull me to my feet.

"I'm sorry," he said. "Look, before you go in, just let
me say this. After Eileen died—well, I tried to put it out
of my mind. Because it hurt too much to think of her; I
knew I wasn't being smart not to face up to it. Once
I actually managed to paint a portrait of her the way I
remembered her."

Now that he was going to let me go, I felt my hostility
recede. The night seemed to press down gently on me.

"I saw the portrait," I said in a low voice. "It's very
good."

He gave no indication that he had heard me. It was
clear that he was trying very hard to explain properly, to
find the right words. "But the portrait was as far as it
went," he said, still holding my hand. "I could picture her
alive, but not dead. And then yesterday, for the first time,
I made myself talk about what had happened, and it was
as though it had just happened. Do you know what I'm
trying to say? It was as though I was having my first real
reaction to her death. I haven't been able to think of
anything else since then. I was awake all last night. You're
right, I've been obsessed. My mind seems to be running
wild."

He shook his head as though he were trying to clear it.
"I'm sorry," he said. "That's really what I'm trying to say.
I had no right to subject you to this."

"It's all right," I said. My anger had changed to sympathy. I felt as I had when I first met him—protective. I wanted to comfort him in some way, but I did not know how. "I'm only sorry that it had to be this way for you."

Our eyes met, and I smiled. In that moment I heard the ringing of a bell and saw the glare of headlights through the trees in the direction of the gatehouse.

"What is it?" I said, my breath catching in my throat, knowing the answer but needing to have him say the word.

"It's an ambulance," Ron murmured in a low voice, his hand tightening on mine. "Something's happened at Pennarth."

When Ron returned to the cottage ten minutes later, Miranda was with him. She was wearing the scarlet robe she had worn when I had seen her that afternoon, and her dark hair was tangled about her haggard face. I stood in the doorway of the kitchen where I had been making tea and watched silently as Ron guided her to a chair. She was weeping quietly, making mewing sounds like a young child, and her dark eyes were glazed as she looked from Ron to me and back again without seeming to really see either of us.

"I found her down by the main gate, trying to wrench it open," he told me. "I couldn't really make much sense out of what she's been saying, but I gather she thought the ambulance should have come in that way, although she must know that they'd use the back approach to the house."

"Did she tell you what's happened?" I demanded.

"The old man's dead," Ron replied. I took a deep breath. Not until that moment did I realize how afraid I had been that somehow something had happened to Paul.

"That's about all the sense I could get out of her," Ron said in a low voice. "Who in God's name *is* she?"

"Paul Randolph's wife," I murmured. "She can't stay here. If his father's dead, he'll be upset enough without having to search for her. She came here the other night, and he was really angry. You'll have to take her up there."

Ron ran one hand through his hair. "I don't know if she'll go," he said. "She seems to be hysterical. Perhaps if we give her some of that tea and you talk to her——"

I poured the tea and laced it with brandy. Miranda drank it greedily and held out her cup for more. I lowered myself onto the chair beside her while Ron went to get it.

"What happened, Miranda?" I asked her softly. "Tell me about it."

She stared at me, slowly focusing her dark eyes. The tears were drying on her thin cheeks now, and when I leaned forward to gently brush her long hair back from her face, she caught my hand and pressed it against her forehead.

"Blood," she said. "I don't like blood."

I felt my throat tighten. "It's all right," I murmured. "You don't have to talk about it if you don't want to."

"I want to know what happened," Ron said in a flat voice. He was standing over her, holding out the cup of tea, but she ignored him.

I shook my head at him in warning. Surely if he knew as much about the household at Pennarth as he seemed to, he must be aware that Paul's wife had suffered a breakdown. Unless that was one thing that had been kept a secret. Since he had asked me who she was, apparently he had not seen her before or talked with anyone from the village who had, but at the very least he must realize from seeing her now that she was in no condition to be pressed.

"It was all over him," Miranda said suddenly in a shrill voice, lowering my hand from her forehead and clutching it beneath both of hers. "He was lying on the floor, and everything was red."

In a few words she had painted too vivid a picture of what she had seen. I shuddered.

"What happened to him?" Ron said. "Come on. You might as well tell us. We have to know what happened if we're going to help you."

He was still holding the cup of tea and brandy in front of her. Without turning to look at him, she struck out with one hand, and the cup shattered against the floor. Ron swore.

"Don't press her," I implored him. "Let me talk to her."

Scowling, he went to the fireplace and leaned against the mantel.

"Whatever happened," I told her in a low voice, "it's all right now. The ambulance is there by now, and there'll be a doctor to see to everything. But you'll have to go back soon, you know. They'll be looking for you."

She was still holding my hand with one of hers, and her nails dug into my skin. "No," she said. "I don't want to go back. They'll blame me."

"No one's going to blame you for anything," I told her, not certain what she meant but realizing the absolute necessity of reassuring her. It was impossible for me to know whether she was in this state because she had been frightened or because she felt her father-in-law's death deeply. I doubted the latter simply on the basis of the attitude I had seen her display toward him that afternoon when she had slipped past him out of the library like a guilty child, but it was possible that she felt some sort of grief.

She was leaning forward now, her face very close to mine. "You don't understand," she whispered. "They'll think I killed him."

"No," I said, aware of a growing helplessness. How could I reassure her when I had only the vaguest notion of what had happened? "No one will think that."

"Ask her what happened," Ron said in a tight voice.

"I'm not supposed to go into his bedroom," Miranda said. Her dark eyes seemed to be pleading with me.

"Was that where you found him?" I asked softly. "In his bedroom?"

"It wasn't my fault," she said. "It wasn't my fault that he fell out of his chair."

"He was lying on the floor when you found him then?"

I hated myself for questioning her in this oblique way, but perhaps it was necessary for her to tell someone. If only I could help her re-create what she had seen in a logical series of mental images, she could cope with the memory. Perhaps once she had told me, she would agree to go back.

"He was all blood," she gasped, inclining her head until her tangled hair veiled her face. "The back of his head was all broken in. It was like a broken egg, and I——"

"It's all right," I crooned. "It's all over now."

"Murder," I heard Ron mutter. "God, they'll raise a hue and cry over this one."

It was clear that he was not talking to me, and I did not answer him. But I shared his sense of shock. The natural death of a man in his eighties was one thing. Murder was another. I knew that I must be certain that it was murder, because if it was, the police would come. There would be questions asked. And if it was murder, I wanted to think about my answers, because Paul would be suspect. As heir to the estate he had the most obvious motive for wanting his father dead.

"Listen to me, Miranda," I said.

She lifted her worn face and looked at me with trustful eyes. It was the most disconcerting thing about her, that childlike attitude, contrasting as sharply as it did with her aging, tormented face.

"I know it isn't pleasant for you to think of this," I said. "But was there any chance that your father-in-law simply happened to fall out of his wheelchair and struck his head on something? The side of a table, perhaps."

I heard Ron give a low laugh, and I moved my chair closer to Miranda. If he were to enrage her as he had when she struck the cup from his hands, there would be no coherent answers from her. Apparently he did not realize this, and I could not take the time to explain it to him.

She was staring at me thoughtfully, her lips moving as

though she were verbalizing something to herself. "I screamed," she said finally. "I screamed when I saw him on the floor, and they all came. Paul was angry with me, you see, because I wasn't supposed to be in that room."

It was, I saw, going to be even more difficult than I had thought to get her to tell me what I wanted to know. I tried another approach.

"Do you remember this afternoon when I came to see Mr. Randolph?" I said.

She nodded, her eyes intent on mine. "We were going to have tea," she said. "But it never came. I shouldn't have taken you to the library, you see. They explained that afterward. I'm not supposed to go to any of his rooms, but I forget." Her lower lip trembled as though she were about to cry.

"Don't think of that," I said gently. "It was a natural mistake for you to make. But after you left, when I was talking to Mr. Randolph, he became excited, and he started to fall out of his chair."

My back was toward Ron, but I could sense that he had moved away from the fireplace and was standing close to us, listening.

"Now," I went on, "that surprised me very much. If your—if Paul hadn't come into the room just at that moment and pulled him back against the chair, he would have toppled out of it. And I would have felt very guilty afterward because I could have possibly prevented him from falling. Do you see that?"

"Yes." She looked at me as though my words had mesmerized her. "Yes, I see that."

"Is that what happened tonight?" I said slowly. "Were you talking to Mr. Randolph, and did he get excited and fall forward? Because if that's what happened, everyone will understand that you couldn't catch him in time. Is that what happened, Miranda? Did he fall and strike his head against something?"

"No." Her voice was so low that I could scarcely hear

her. "No!" she repeated the denial as she uncoiled herself from the chair and rose, dropping my hand. "No!" she screamed. "He was lying on the floor when I looked into the room. The door was open. I wouldn't have gone in if it hadn't been open and he hadn't been on the floor and there hadn't been all that blood! It's on my dress. Don't you see it? I'm all dirty with it!"

She tore at the scarlet gown, and I saw, along the hem, black streaks. I raised my eyes and found her staring at me strangely.

"You think I did it, don't you?" she demanded. "You and he." She pointed at Ron. "You hate me like all the others. You want to have me put away. You're going to tell the police I killed him!"

"No," I said. "No, Miranda. No one murdered him."

"He didn't hit his head against anything!" she cried, staring about her blindly. "Someone hit him. With the hammer. A big hammer. It was slippery with blood. I tried to pick it up, but it was all slippery!"

She pushed the palms of her hands down the side of her body as though she were trying to wipe them clean. "Kill!" she cried. "They wanted to kill him! They came up behind him and hit his head with the hammer! I saw—"

Her voice culminated in a scream, and suddenly Ron had her by the shoulders and was shaking her back and forth. I saw her go limp and sway against him. "Who?" he shouted. "Who did you see?"

She was a big woman, too heavy for him to support. When she let herself slump, he had no choice but to lower her back into the chair. Her eyes were closed, and she was breathing heavily.

"Let her alone," I said softly. "Don't ask her any more questions."

"But she knows——"

"We don't know what she knows. She's hysterical. None of this may be true."

"It's true." He straightened himself, and our eyes met

and held. "It's true, and you know it. The question is, what are we going to do about it?"

"Do about it?" I stared at him, bewildered. "It's not our affair."

"The police may choose to make it our affair," Ron said.

"Listen, Ron," I murmured, "the only thing that concerns us now is getting Miranda back to the house. Paul was worried enough when she came here the other night. Now that there's been a murder—*if* there has been one— he'll be doubly upset when he finds she isn't in the house."

"It matters a good deal to you how he feels, doesn't it?" Ron said in a flat voice.

I ignored the comment. There was no time now to explain to him how I felt about either him or Paul. Perhaps that was something I did not even understand myself. "Miranda," I said softly, "it's time for you to go back to Pennarth."

When I spoke, her eyes were still closed. Now she opened them in response to my words. Her gaze was flat and blank. "No," she said, "I'm not going."

For some strange reason nothing that had happened that night disturbed me as much as her flat refusal. I knew I could not bear to have her all night in this house.

"Talk to her," I said shrilly. "Tell her you'll go with her."

"That wouldn't be the truth," Ron said. "I'm sorry, Sara, but I have no intention of going up to that house. Particularly tonight."

"All right." I took a deep breath. "But you can at least take Paul a message to let him know where she is."

Ron shook his head and turned toward the door.

"Why?" I demanded. "Why won't you do this?"

"I should think it would be obvious," he said, his hand on the knob of the door. "I was involved in the affairs of these—these people once, and I don't want to be involved again. The police are up there. If I turn up with Paul

Randolph's wife, or even if I simply come with a message saying where she is, I'll be questioned."

"All right," I said. "So you're questioned. I said a while ago that both of us probably would be anyway. If there has been a murder——"

"You're still holding on to the idea that perhaps nothing has really happened up at that house, aren't you?" He turned; his blue eyes were very bright. They seemed to delve into me. "Sara, why don't you look life in the face? You thought you could come here and bury yourself away, didn't you? You must have realized by now that it's not going to be as simple as that. Life isn't ever simple. I accepted that a long time ago. The only thing you can try to do is to keep yourself as uninvolved as you can in the messes other people make."

"That's an interesting philosophy," I said wearily. "But it doesn't solve the problem of Miranda, does it?"

"That's not my problem. Can't you understand?"

For a moment we stared at one another in silence, then he turned back toward the door. In that moment we both heard the sound of men's voices outside. With a quick movement Ron stepped into the darkened kitchen, pushed aside one of the red curtains, then let it drop in place again.

"It's the police," he said. "I'm leaving by the boxroom. And I advise you not to mention the fact."

"They'll have to know that you were here."

The voices were closer now. Ron's face was drawn and pale, his eyes fastened on mine.

"You seem to have the interest of Paul Randolph a good deal at heart," he said. "I could tell the police a thing or two about him if I was asked. Okay. So she may tell them I was here." He pointed at Miranda who was breathing deeply again as though asleep. "If she can make that much sense, perhaps she will. I'll cope with that when the time comes. But I'm telling you that it's better for everyone concerned if I'm not involved."

I did not understand him. A knock sounded on the door, and I rose and slowly made my way toward it. I heard the click of the boxroom door and knew that Ron was gone. Opening the front door, I found two uniformed policemen standing on the stone step, and behind them Enoch Lessing, bent low over his cane.

"Miss Grey?" one of the officers said. He was a young man with a fresh country face. "We're looking for Mrs. Randolph. Her husband thought she might be with you."

I opened the door wider, my eyes on Enoch. Why, I wondered, did he not raise his head and look at me? Why had he come?

"Yes," I said. "She's here."

The first officer stepped past me into the room. Immediately Miranda began to scream. I turned and saw her propel herself out of the chair and into a corner, where she crouched like an animal. "No!" she screamed. "No!"

"I told you that you'd better let me handle this, officer," Enoch Lessing said in his hoarse voice. "Now, if you'll let me speak to Miss Grey alone."

The police officer who had come inside the cottage went back onto the step, his round face flushed. As soon as he was out of her sight, Miranda stopped screaming. I limped down onto the path and took Enoch's arm. For the first time since he had come, he raised his great white head and looked at me.

"Do you think you can convince her to come back to the house?" he asked in a low voice. "You know what's happened, don't you?"

"She told me that Mr. Randolph is dead."

"Very well. Now listen, my dear. She's upset, that's clear."

"She doesn't want to go back there."

"That's natural enough. But she'll feel better about it if you come with her."

"But I can't——" I began.

"You'll plan to spend at least one night," Enoch said as

though the matter were settled. "That's what Paul wants. She's talked a good deal about you since she came here the other time. She trusts you. Paul wants her to have someone she cares about with her, because it looks as though he may be accused of his father's murder."

An hour later Miranda allowed me to put her to bed. We had arrived at Pennarth within fifteen minutes of the time the police had knocked on my door.

The police officers and Enoch had waited outside the door while I talked to Miranda. Surprisingly, she had made no protest when she heard that I intended to return home with her. She had ignored the two policemen and Enoch, walking in front of them, her arm in mine, down the path to where the police car was parked by the gate.

All the rooms of the main part of the house were alight when we drove up to the back entrance. Enoch did not speak during the drive, nor did Miranda, but she gripped my hand with icy fingers and did not release me as Enoch led the way into the house and up a flight of narrow stairs to the second floor.

The housekeeper was waiting by the door to Miranda's bedroom, her face expressionless. She held the door open for us without speaking, although after it was closed, I heard her voice rise angrily in response to something Enoch had said.

I told Miranda that I thought she should go to bed. She complied readily, slipping the scarlet robe over her head with the unself-consciousness of a child. In contrast to her lined, haggard face, her body was firm and smooth-skinned. A blue-silk nightgown was laid out on the bed, and I turned the covers down as she put it on. She went to the vanity table then and sat on the small gilt stool in front of it.

"Paul always brushes my hair before I go to bed," she said happily. "But tonight you will do that, won't you? I won't have to see anyone but you."

I brushed the tangles from the long black hair as she leaned her head back, her eyes half closed as though she were totally absorbed in the sensation. Apparently she had been able to put what had happened out of her mind. I wished that I could do the same.

I tried to concentrate on the regular movement of my arm as I brought the brush down from the top of her head to the ends of that long dark hair and back again. I made myself think of my own weariness and of the ache in my ankle. As I looked at the room and saw it reflected in the mirror, I tried to fasten my mind on the details of the flower pattern of the delicate wallpaper, the elegance of the white French provincial furniture, the bed with its white canopied top and the white ruffles that hid its base. The sheets were pink and the coverlet as well.

It was the room of a dainty feminine woman, or perhaps of a young girl. There was nothing about it that seemed to relate to the woman who sat in front of me with her tilted face set in an expression of sensuous enjoyment. Did this room reflect what Paul had wanted her to be? I wondered. Or had this been what she once was?

Paul. It was impossible to keep thoughts of him from my mind. There was no sign of his presence in this room, and I hated the relief that it brought me. But this woman *was* his wife. I would be a fool to forget that. Every night he stood where I was standing and ran this brush through her thick hair. He was her husband, and yet she had not asked to see him. In fact, she seemed glad that tonight I was doing this for her instead of him. Whatever the nature of their relationship, it was too complex for me to imagine. I knew only that when Enoch told me Paul might be accused of the murder of his father, my heart seemed to constrict.

Miranda appeared to be almost asleep when I ran the brush through her hair for the last time. She let me lead her to the bed and tuck her in, her hair fanning out on the pillow. The lights were muted under pink shades, and as she lay there, smiling up at me, I realized with a pang how beautiful she once had been.

"And now," she said drowsily, "you must ring that bell, and Grace will bring me my warm milk and my pill. I can't sleep without my pill."

There was a white button set in the wall near the head of the bed, but I had not had time to push it when the door opened and the housekeeper appeared bearing a silver tray. Instantly Miranda became agitated.

"Don't let her come inside," she whispered. "I don't want her here."

I went to get the tray, limping across the room. "Your bedroom is ready, miss," the housekeeper said tonelessly as I took the tray from her. "It adjoins this room. Mr. Randolph has asked that you keep the door ajar during the night."

As I took the tray from her, she pointed to a door beside the vanity table and left, stiff-backed, radiating disapproval. The milk drunk and the pill taken, Miranda began to hum to herself, and I felt free to leave her. Opening the door beside the vanity table, I was startled to find myself in what was obviously Paul's bedroom.

His touch was everywhere. The furniture was quite unlike anything one would expect to find in a house like this—sleek and modern with smooth lines and flat surfaces bare of everything except the most fundamental possessions. The bed, so large that it must have been custom-made, was set low to the floor. A single lamp was burning on a table by one of the long windows, but there were small lights aglow over the paintings that lined the walls, all of them stark cubist work with colors that seemed to leap from the canvases. I stood motionless, the door nearly closed behind me, and abandoned myself to the atmosphere of the place, so different from that of the cottage but so strangely appealing that it took my breath away.

Suddenly someone rose from the armchair that faced the fireplace. My first impression was that it must be Paul, and I started forward, his name on my lips. Then I saw Enoch's mass of white hair and his cherub's face and was not certain whether the emotion that drove itself through me was that of disappointment or relief.

"I hope you don't mind finding me here, my dear," he puffed, straightening himself with an effort. "But I guessed that all of this must have come as rather a shock to you, and I thought you might want to talk a bit before you retired. Also, I may as well confess, it was not my idea entirely. Paul wanted to be certain that you were all right."

The room was long, and standing at the farther end of it, we were far enough from the door to Miranda's bedroom so that she would not hear our voices. With a courtly gesture Enoch waved me into the chair he had vacated and indicated the low table in front of me on which were set a decanter of port and two wineglasses.

"The wine was my idea entirely," he said, grinning mischievously. "We'll have a cozy few minutes together, and then I'll let you go to sleep. No, this straight-backed chair is fine. There. Now we can talk quite quietly together. If you'll do the honors. . . ."

I poured the wine, and we raised our glasses to one another. It was simply another incredible part of an incredible day, and as the port warmed my throat, I leaned back and let myself begin to relax. I had not known this old man long. I had had only two conversations with him, yet somehow I felt that he knew me better than I knew myself. If Ron Farrow's personality struck against mine abrasively, this man touched me like cotton wool.

"And now," he said, touching the tips of his gnarled fingers together and peering over them at me inquisitively, "there must be a good many questions you would like to ask. Paul wanted me to explain everything to you—as much, that is, as can be explained."

"Where is he now?"

I realized as soon as I had uttered the words that they constituted the most important question I could ask. The matter of precisely what had happened to old Mr. Randolph could wait until later. I surprised myself, but I did not appear to have surprised Enoch.

"He is with the police," he said soberly. "And it is likely that he will be kept with them for some time. That is one of the reasons why he wanted you to return to Pennarth with his wife. She will usually allow no one here close to her except her husband. He had no way of knowing what emotional state she would be in, but he thought that in his absence it would be best if you were with her. And he was right. I see that now. I had not expected her to return here as quietly as she did."

"You said that was one reason why he wanted me to return," I said in a low voice, raising the glass to my lips. "What were the others?"

"Only one other, my dear. He wanted to be assured of your safety. He is convinced, you see, that no one in this household is capable of having done to his father what—what was done. Therefore, he assumes that the murderer is somewhere about the estate. He did not want you to be alone at the cottage. Young Paul and I have differed over the years on a great many things, although my position has, of course, dictated that I not speak out. But about this matter, I could not be in more complete agreement."

For a moment I did not speak. Perhaps later I would blame myself for having it mean so much to me that Paul had worried about me. Later I might blame myself for a good many things. Agreeing to come here might be one of them, but now the only thing that seemed to matter was that Paul cared about my safety and that, as a result, I was under the same roof with him.

"Perhaps you'd like to ask a few questions about the murder," Enoch murmured with a whimsical smile.

I knew why he was amused. By asking first about Paul I had made it all too clear where my real interests lay. It pleased me that there was no need for me to practice hypocrisy with this old man. He understood that old Mr.

Randolph had meant nothing to me. Or perhaps that was not quite true. Paul's father had been a threat. I had not liked him. I had been, to some degree, afraid of him. From what I had seen and from what Paul had told me, I thought it better, perhaps, that he was dead. But he should have died a natural death. Ron had told me that I would try to reject the idea of murder to the last, and it was so. I found it difficult to phrase any questions concerning what had happened here, because I did not want to hear the answers.

"Tell me what happened," I said in a low voice.

Enoch pouched his face reflectively. "You may think this odd of me," he said, "but I'd really like to hear what Miranda told you. Her version through your lips, as it were."

I drained the glass and poured myself another from the crystal decanter, watching the ruby richness of the port climb to the rim.

"She was down at the gate when the ambulance went by, apparently," I said. "Ron—"

I broke off. Enoch leaned forward with an effort in his chair and cupped his hand around one ear. "You'll have to speak up a bit, my dear," he said. "I'm getting a bit deaf in my old age. I didn't catch that last bit."

I realized with a flash of intuition that he had. He had heard me say Ron's name, and he realized that once having uttered it, I was disconcerted. He was giving me a chance to backtrack. Remembering Ron's threat about the harm that he could do Paul, I did. Later, perhaps, I would tell someone about his visit. Perhaps the police if they interviewed me. Perhaps Paul. Perhaps even Enoch. But not now. I told myself that part of the story did not matter.

"I—I said that I saw the lights of the ambulance," I went on, "and directly after that Miranda appeared at the door. It must have been about eleven. I—I was about to go to bed. My ankle——"

"Paul told me about that," Enoch said. I had not raised my voice, but it was obvious that he was hearing what I said quite distinctly. "That was another reason he wanted you here. Does it pain you now?"

"No," I said truthfully. "Not as long as I'm sitting down. It will probably be all right by tomorrow."

"I'm glad of that. Now, my dear, you were saying. . . ."

"Miranda came to the door," I said, taking a deep breath. "She was quite upset. At first it was difficult to make any sense out of what she was saying, but I gathered that Mr. Randolph was dead and that she had found him lying on the floor of his bedroom."

"Yes. Go on."

"She said that there was a great deal of blood. I took it that his head was—"

"Was battered in. Yes. That's quite right, my dear."

"It couldn't have been an accident?" I demanded in sudden desperation. "Isn't it possible that he could have fallen out of the wheelchair and struck his head on something?"

Enoch shook his white-thatched head slowly. "No," he replied. "I saw the body. There is no question of its being an accident, I'm afraid. Someone quite deliberately battered his head with a hammer. The weapon was there. An ordinary hammer covered with his blood and bits of his hair and skull. The police have it now. I'm sorry, my dear. This isn't pleasant for you. Are you all right?"

I realized I must be pale. When he had spoken of the hammer and the blood and hair, I had felt the blood draining from my face. My imagination had conjured up too readily the picture Enoch painted. But there was more than that. There was a certain relish in the way he described the body that sickened me. I could understand that this old man might be glad that another man who had, for so many years, been his tyrant as well as his master was dead, but not glad that he had been brutally murdered. And what right did I have, really, to think that Mr. Randolph had tyrannized his valet for more than half a century? That was the danger of imagination.

The man who hunched himself in the chair beside me might never have had any cause to hate anyone but himself, and that for his lack of decision. Perhaps, although he had written to Miss Randolph every day for many, many years, he had been relieved that he had not followed and married her. For all I knew, he might have been quite content to remain here as a servant. Appealing as I found him, his will might be weak.

For the past few years he had been treated generously as a pensioner. In all his life he might have had no real reason to hate Mr. Randolph, but if that were so, why was it that he exhibited something close to pleasure in the violence of his master's death? His voice roused me, and I saw that he was peering at me myopically.

"We won't speak again of that part of it," he assured me hoarsely. "What else did Miranda tell you?"

"Nothing else," I said and only then remembered she had hinted that she had seen the murder committed. How had she put it? "They came up behind him and hit his head with the hammer. I saw—" That, at least, was what I remembered. But had she really meant that she had seen the murderer? Nothing else she had said indicated that. I could not quote her, uncertain as I was that I had even remembered her words exactly. "No," I went on. "Nothing else. Except that she seemed to think she would be blamed."

"Ah!" Enoch inclined his great head. His eyes peered up at me from under the fringe of white hair. "And why do you think she expected to be blamed?"

"Because she was the one who found him," I said slowly. "If you're implying that she might have been responsible, I don't believe that. She made a good deal of the fact that she wasn't supposed to be in his room. But I don't think that she did go in it until she saw the body through the open door."

"I expect that she will be more coherent tomorrow," Enoch murmured heavily. "Paul had to be very specific about the nature of her illness before he could convince the police not to interview her tonight. I expect that her reaction when she saw the officers who came down to the cottage with me to fetch her may have been convincing. No doubt they have already told the inspector how she screamed."

I sipped my wine and then, suddenly finding no pleasure in its taste, set it down on the table in front of me.

"What exactly is wrong with her?" I inquired carefully.

The old man shook his head. "Technically, I don't know. As you probably realize, neither the elder Mr. Randolph nor Mr. Paul chose to discuss the matter with me." The bitterness in his voice seemed to drag the words back into his throat. I leaned forward to hear him. "However," he went on more brightly, "I have developed excellent powers of observation over the years. When Paul first brought his wife here, she was a completely different personality than she has become. A rather aristocratic woman. There was a—how shall I put it?—a certain delicacy about her."

I thought of the sprigged wallpaper in Miranda's bedroom and the white-ruffled frills about the bed. The room had been decorated at her choice, then, and not because Paul wanted to make her into something she was not. It had been absurd of me to think that of him. But how terrible for him to have married one sort of woman and found himself now tied to quite another personality. I shook my head. It would be just as well if I did not concern myself with how Paul felt or did not feel about the woman who lay sleeping in the next room.

Sleeping? I had left her awake. Perhaps she was awake still. Perhaps she had even crept out of the room to escape for a second time that night. Or she might well be listening at the door. Her bedroom was thickly carpeted, as was this room. Paul had appointed me her guardian for the night. Until now I had forgotten that.

Murmuring an explanation to Enoch, I rose and limped to farther end of the room. Without opening the door wider I could see the bed. The single lamp I had left burning illuminated Miranda's thick dark hair spread on the pillow. I sighed my relief and returned to my chair.

"You don't have to be concerned about her having left the house again," Enoch said. "The housekeeper was given orders to bolt the door on the outside. A necessary precaution, you understand." He was attempting to pour himself another glass of port, but his hand shook so much that I took the decanter away from him and poured the wine myself.

"You were talking about her condition," I reminded him.

"Ah, yes. Well, when she came here, she was quite a different person than she appears to be today. There were rumors that she had had a nervous breakdown in London."

I nodded. That was what Paul had told me.

"For about a year after she came here," Enoch said reflectively, "she seemed to improve. Eileen Randolph was living then, you know. She and the girl were great friends. And then Eileen was sent away to school. She was nearly eighteen, and her father said it was time that she saw something of the world."

His eyes were fastened on the glass in his hand. There was no way I could tell whether or not he believed that had been the reason Eileen had been sent away or whether what Ron had said was true—that she had been banished from Pennarth to keep her from seeing him.

"And then, of course," Enoch said heavily, "the girl returned. Shortly afterward there was an accident." He lifted his gaze and met my eyes. I kept my face expressionless. There was no need for him to know now how much I had been told about Eileen. "At all events," he went on, "the girl died. Tragically. After that Miranda changed. She aged suddenly. Put on weight. Began to wear odd clothing. And, increasingly, to act in a peculiar manner."

"Tell me."

Enoch seemed disinclined to indulge me. "You've seen her," he said, his old eyes watchful. "You know what she's like. Passionate. Unreasonable. Incoherent at times. Capable of drawing into her own world and isolating herself from everyone."

Did she, I wondered, often isolate herself from Paul? Probably. She had gone with him that first night when he had come to the cottage searching for her, but she had kept herself apart. She had not even greeted him. And yet every night before she went to bed he brushed her hair. It was strange that that thought should give me so much pain.

"Perhaps," Enoch said, his eyes still fastened on me curiously, "you're wondering, in the light of what's happened here, if she is ever violent. I suppose I should have to say that she is. Now and then she flares into a temper and breaks things. That was the reason the elder Mr. Randolph barred her from his particular rooms, the library, the bedroom. That and the fact that he could not stand the sight of her."

I felt a sudden surge of pity for the woman lying asleep in the other room. Surely everyone here must realize that it was not her fault that she was tormented.

"Have doctors been consulted?" I asked wearily. "Can't anything be done?"

"From what I've overheard," Enoch said, "a number of specialists have suggested that she be hospitalized."

"Committed?"

"That's not a very pleasant word, is it? But yes— committed. Apparently Paul refuses, since they cannot guarantee her recovery. He feels some sort of personal responsibility to care for her himself."

"She hates it here."

"Perhaps she does. But then she might find any place a prison. I have no reason to believe that she would find a mental hospital more pleasant. Of course, medication has been prescribed. When she's at her worst, she can be soothed artificially. Tell me, are you so curious about her because it has occurred to you that she might be responsible for Mr. Randolph's death?"

I would have expected the question to have taken me by surprise, but somehow it did not. Perhaps, subconsciously, that was what I wanted to believe. The thought, faced directly, appalled me.

"Do you—do you think she is capable of—"

"Murder? Yes, I expect all of us are capable of that in the end." Enoch bowed his head. "And Miranda had a motive of sorts to want him dead. It was because of his father that Paul remained here. She may have thought that once her father-in-law was dead——"

Now was the time to say it. "But you said—when you came to the cottage, you said that the police suspect Paul."

"That matters to you, doesn't it?" the old man said. His voice was gentle, as though he were consoling me. "I must admit that when you two went off together this afternoon, I thought you might find you had more in common, let us say, than you suspected."

I felt myself flush. "There's nothing very complicated about it," I said. "I simply don't think he could have killed his father or anyone."

"He had an excellent motive," Enoch reminded me. "He gave up his professional life in London because his father demanded it. Paul is forty, you know. It isn't pleasant for a man of that age to be dependent on the whims of an arbitrary old man. I know. I've watched him chafe under it for years. And I have some personal experience to draw from. Not that that matters. But the fact remains that now that his father is dead, the son is free. Free and very rich. That's a powerful combination, my dear."

"You sound as though you were convinced he's guilty," I said angrily. "Have the police talked to you? Did you tell them what you've told me?"

"No." The old man shook his head slowly. "In the first place the inspector is a pragmatic man, as you will doubt-

less see for yourself. He doesn't ask for speculation. At
this point he's more concerned with the problem of which
of us had the means and opportunity to have committed
this—this murder. The body was found at ten thirty, apparently. At least that was when Mrs. Aiken heard Miranda scream. She came up the stairs to see what was
wrong at the same time that Miranda ran down them and
out of the house.

"The police were called immediately. And a doctor.
They arrived approximately fifteen minutes later. It was
the doctor's opinion that the elder Mr. Randolph had been
dead for less than an hour at that time. Therefore, it is to
be supposed that the inspector would be interested in es-
tablishing where each one of us was at about ten o'clock."

Breathing became a conscious effort for me, something
that always happened when I was nervous. But why
should I be tense? All of this did not concern me. It did
not *really* concern me.

"And where were you?" I asked.

Enoch rubbed his forehead with one age-freckled hand.
Somehow the gesture seemed to indicate something that I
had had no indication of before, that he was under great
strain. For the first time since we had begun to talk, I
remembered his age. It was so easy to forget that Enoch
was an old man, despite his shuffling walk and his
hunched shoulders.

"Perhaps," I said, "you'd rather not talk about it."

"No, my dear. Paul wanted you to know all there is to
know about this. All that's left is the question of what I
believe the police refer to as alibis. The awkward thing is
that none of us has one. Our habits and the time of night
dictated that. I was in my sitting room, as I always am at
that hour, dozing a bit, I assume. Lately I seem to doze a
good deal. The first I knew that anything out of the way
had happened was when I heard Miranda scream. I didn't
react, not at first. It all became part of a dream, you see.
But apparently the housekeeper hurried to see what was
wrong."

"Where was she?"

"In the kitchen. It's usual for her to be there at that time of night, preparing Mr. Randolph's hot milk. And Miranda's. She claims to have run down the corridor and——"

"Past your sitting room?"

"Yes. She must have, since she went up the front stairs. That was when she met Miranda running down them. Why do you ask?"

"Did you hear her?"

Enoch shook his head. "The police asked me that. I couldn't tell them. The scream was part of the dream, you see, and I didn't really awake until I heard people moving about and talking rather loudly in the main part of the house."

"What people?"

"The housekeeper. And Paul. And one of the two maids who live in. The maid was terribly upset, poor thing. I went out into the main hall and found them there at the foot of the stairs. It seems that Paul had been in his own den downstairs, reading. At least that was what he told the police. He had music playing on the stereo, and it seems that he didn't know that anything was wrong until the housekeeper knocked on the door. By the time I joined them, he had been upstairs to verify what she had told him and then had come down to call the police, explaining what had happened. I can tell you that it came as a shock to me."

"What about Miranda?"

The old man threw me a confused glance. "What do you mean?"

"Where was she at ten o'clock?"

"We don't know that, do we?" Enoch reminded me. "The police have not questioned her yet, and directly after finding the body, she left the house. Did she mention to you——"

"No," I said. "She simply told me that she was passing by her father-in-law's bedroom and that she looked through the open door and saw him lying on the floor in a pool of blood."

"Then probably she had been in her bedroom," Enoch said.

"Is that where she usually spends her evenings?"

"It depends," Enoch said thoughtfully. "Lately she's been going through a rather active period, which means that she's likely to pace through the house like a restless cat. She rarely wears shoes, you know, when she's inside, and she has often passed me in the hallway without my knowing that she was anywhere around. When she's feeling like that, no one knows where she may turn up.

"She went through a period when she insisted upon going into the wing. There's nothing there, you know. Bare rooms. Bricked-up windows. A terrible place. And yet she would walk there in the dark. Until Paul became afraid that she might hurt herself in some way and had the doors locked.

"It was the same with the tower. Soon after Eileen died she was found there. At the top. It was all that Paul could do to convince her to come down. There's a tower room, you see, at the top of the stone stairs, and she somehow got it into her head that she wanted to live there. Ah, well, she's quite rational at times. Quite subdued, one might say."

"I suppose," I said in a low voice, "that the tower is kept locked now."

"Certainly. There were obviously some places that she should not be allowed to go."

A wave of sadness swept over me. Everywhere, for Miranda, there must be locked doors. She was locked in her bedroom now. And there were rooms in the main house into which she must not go. I remembered the look in her dark eyes when her father-in-law had found her with me in the library—his library. Now that he was dead there would be fewer restrictions. Perhaps in the confusion of her mind that much had been clear. Perhaps she had

had good reason to want him dead, representing, as he did, forbidden rooms and the total imprisonment of the house itself. Now Paul would be able to leave Pennarth if he liked.

Had Miranda thought of that? I wondered. Had she found the hammer somewhere in her wanderings tonight and later found an old man she hated sitting alone and helpless in his bedroom? Had it seemed to her a simple thing to strike at him? I shivered. It was just as well not to think of what might have happened. Let me, like the inspector, consider only the facts.

"And so," I said, "at the time Mr. Randolph was killed, Miranda may have been in her bedroom or roaming the house, Paul in the downstairs study, Mrs. Atkins in the kitchen, you in your sitting room, and the maids?"

"They were in their third-floor bedrooms," Enoch said. "Together. They alone have alibis. One of them, the more courageous, came downstairs when she heard the commotion. The other stayed cowering in her bed."

"And Mr. Randolph?" I said. "What was he doing in his bedroom alone? Surely a helpless man. . . ."

"He preferred to spend his evenings alone in his library on the second floor," Enoch told me. "I believe that was where you talked with him earlier today."

I nodded. Could it have been today? So much had happened that it seemed as though I had last seen that stiff white skeletal face a year ago. It was difficult to think of all the burning intensity, that immobilized determination gone. Where was his body? I wondered. Still in the house or already on its way to a morgue? And where was Paul? Was he somewhere in the house talking still to the police? Or had he been arrested? No, that was absurd. They could not arrest him unless there was more evidence of his guilt than Enoch had indicated. After all, no one had been with anyone else except the two maids. Anyone could have raised that hammer and brought it down on the back of the old man's head. It would have been only a matter of minutes. The old man beside me was still talking. I must be more tired than I realized if I could not keep my mind on what he was saying.

"The elder Mr. Randolph," Enoch explained, "was in the habit of ringing his bell when he was ready to retire for the night. Often, as apparently happened tonight, he pushed himself into his bedroom. It's only one door down from the library, and he managed the wheelchair with considerable facility. He liked to do as much as he could for himself."

I remembered the way he had propelled himself into the library to meet me and the helpless way in which he had later fallen forward in his chair. I had no reason to feel much sympathy for Paul's father, considering the way he had treated me, but I recognized something of the agony it must have been for a man accustomed to live his own life in precisely the way he wished to live it to be at the mercy of others even for the simplest of activities.

"But tonight," I said, "he apparently didn't ring the bell before he left the library."

"There was nothing unusual about that," Enoch assured me, his old voice gone hoarse from so much talking. "Often he would ring from the bedroom."

"What usually happened then? Did the house-keeper——"

"It was not the housekeeper he called. There were bells connected to the kitchen, naturally, as there are in all the upstairs rooms, but he could also contact Paul in his den downstairs. It was Paul who put him to bed and gave him his medicine."

There was, I thought, more than one sort of tyranny. For the old man it had been the tyranny of the flesh. For Paul that of filial responsibility. "Why wasn't a nurse employed?" I demanded.

"The elder Mr. Randolph disliked strangers," Enoch replied slowly. "Surely you must be aware of that. Paul did nearly everything for him. Or has for the past few years.

There was a time when I could be of a good deal of assistance. But as you see me now. . . ."

I looked at him closely. At some time during our conversation his face had lost its baby plumpness, and now the skin seemed to hang in folds about his mouth and eyes. "You're tired," I said. "You must forgive me for keeping you so long."

Enoch puffed his way out of the chair, and I took his arm. We were a strange pair as I saw us in a mirror, limping and hunching our way to the door that led to the corridor.

"It only remains for me to thank you for coming," the old man said formally as we stood facing one another in parting. "We need you here. Paul in particular. It will be a relief to him to know that Miranda responds to you as she does."

"But where will he sleep?" I said, suddenly aware that I was usurping my host's bedroom.

"If he sleeps at all," Enoch said, "it will be in the den. There's a daybed there."

"Why do you put it that way?" I demanded, not trying to hide my urgency. " 'If he sleeps at all.' You don't really think the police will arrest him, do you?"

"We can hope they will not be as arbitrary as all that," Enoch said, patting my hand. "The inspector seems a sensible man."

"But when you asked me to come here, you said it looked very much as though he would be accused of his father's murder."

For the first time that evening the impish smile lit up the old man's face. "I may have put it rather strongly, my dear," he said. "In fact I know that I did. But I wanted you here. Quite apart from the question of Miranda, there's the fact that none of us who were in this house when the elder Mr. Randolph was killed quite trust one another anymore. At least, my child, we can be sure of you."

I slept deeply, and if there were dreams, I no longer remembered them when I woke to find Miranda, wearing her blue nightgown and a purple fringed shawl over her head, pulling back the brown drapes from the windows disclosing a wall of morning fog, which pressed itself flat and impenetrable against the glass.

"Isn't it lovely?" she said, hurrying across the room to fling herself down on the side of the bed. "After breakfast we can go out and walk in it. Paul won't let me go out alone when it's like this, but he won't mind if I'm with you."

Perhaps it was the gray whiteness of the light, but her face looked less haggard than it had the night before. For the first time since I had met her, her cheeks had a touch of color, and her eyes were happy. She pushed back the shawl, releasing the waves of black hair on her shoulders.

"Can you stay forever?" she asked me. "I'd like it very much if you would stay forever."

I have never been able to awaken rapidly, and in this case there was the matter of finding myself in a strange bed, not to mention the struggle to remember everything that had happened the day before. There was something overpowering about the alertness of this woman who had decided, so wholeheartedly, to adopt me as her friend. I mumbled something incoherent about being glad and pushed myself up against the pillows—Paul's pillows.

"Isn't it nice that we can go downstairs for breakfast today?" Miranda continued rapidly. "Usually, you know, I must have breakfast brought up to my room, but today is different."

"Why?" I said, yawning.

Instantly her smile fled, and her face became dour and sullen. "You know," she said.

"Because I'm here?"

"Not that."

It was as though we were playing a game that displeased her. Obviously I had missed some clue. I tried to pull my sleep-clogged brain together. Why should it have been necessary in the past for her to eat in her room? What had changed since yesterday? If it were not my coming here. . . .

"*He* didn't like to have me around when he had breakfast," Miranda said, rising from the bed and beginning to pace the floor, rubbing her hands together. The shawl had fallen to the carpet, and I could see the loose flesh at the top of her arms. Enoch had said last night that Paul was forty. Was she, I wondered, older than he? And what did it matter anyway? Something had upset her, and it was up to me to quiet her before the whole day went awry.

"Who didn't want you around?" I demanded, throwing off the covers.

"You know." Again she threw me that tight, sullen glance.

And suddenly I did know. She meant Paul. She hated him. It was there in her eyes. She hated and resented him.

"It's only because you're here that I can eat downstairs," she said with suddenly rising hostility. "He wants to see you, so he'll put up with me as well. Don't think that I don't know what's going on. Don't think—"

Suddenly she stopped and shook her head. Her eyes had the bewildered look of one who finds himself in a strange place. I decided to ignore what she had just said, because it was possible that she had already forgotten that she had said it.

"You're right," I said. "It's going to be much more fun to have breakfast downstairs." I rose as I spoke and found that my ankle was no longer paining me.

"And lunch?" Miranda said. "Can I have lunch downstairs, too?" She looked at me expectantly, as a child looks who wants to be reminded of a coming treat. Her hostility had totally disappeared.

"Lunch, too!" I said with a gaiety I did not feel. "But first we get dressed."

Miranda pursed her lips. "I think," she said, "that I'll go down like this. I can do anything I want to now."

It was too early in the morning for this sort of non-sense, but I knew, or thought I knew, that she was not deliberately being difficult. "I don't blame you for wanting to wear your nightgown downstairs," I said, "because it's lovely, but mine is rather old, and I'd like to change."

Obviously the idea that if she went downstairs dishabille, I should have to do the same appealed to her. She preened herself in front of the mirror, tossing back her dark hair. "All right," she said brightly. "You're gown *is* shabby, isn't it? Would you like me to give you one of mine?"

"It would be much too big," I said, going to stand beside her. We made an odd picture in the mirror, she so much taller than I, an older woman verging on the heavy-set, her dark skin and hair contrasting so markedly with my own paleness. I breathed a sigh of relief as she broke into laughter. There was nothing hysterical about her reaction. She was simply amused. And then with disconcerting abruptness she became silent. Her eyes narrowed as she assessed me closely in the glass.

"Wait!" she said and half walked, half ran into her bedroom.

In a moment she was back, holding a wisp of a night-gown in front of her, a pale-gray piece of transparency, far too small for it to have been hers.

"You can have this," she said excitedly. "And I have lots of other things. They'll all fit you. When you stood beside me, I could see that you were just her size."

A chill of premonition came over me. "Whose clothes are you talking about?" I asked, trying to be casual, digging about in my nightcase for my sponge and comb.

"Eileen's, of course," Miranda said. She came up to me and tried to push the nightgown into my hands. "Take it," she said in a loud voice. "I want you to take it!"

"Miranda!"

She leaped to her feet. Beyond her, in the doorway of her bedroom, I saw Paul. He was wearing gray slacks and a blue sweater. His face was pale, and there were dark circles under his eyes. His mouth was set in that same grim expression I had noticed when he had come to my cottage that first night to take Miranda home. This time, as then, he ignored me.

"You'll want to change for breakfast downstairs," he said to his wife in a controlled voice. "I've run your bath."

She went toward him, moving like an automaton, clutching the nightgown to her. When she reached the door, he took it from her, bending back her fingers to force her to release the cloth. Without speaking she passed by him, her shoulders slumping, and disappeared into her own room.

"It's Eileen's," I said in a low voice because he remained standing where he was, staring at what was in his hands. "She thought it might fit me."

"I'm sorry." The words seemed forced from his throat. "I didn't realize that she had—that she had this."

"She spoke as though she had all your sister's clothing," I said.

I wanted to make him look at me. It had hurt too much to be ignored. Whatever the consequences, I did not want us to slip back into our first relationship, which had been no real relationship at all. After all, he had asked that I come here, and I wanted to help him. We would have to be open with one another if I were to do that. There was no use hiding anything, no matter how awkward it might be.

"I'm sorry," he said again. For a moment his eyes met mine. "Come downstairs when you're ready. The dining room is to the right of the great hall." He turned toward the door. "How has she been?"

"She was calm last night, as soon as we left the cottage."

"Enoch told me that."

I wished that he would turn and face me. "And this morning she seemed quite happy."

"I heard her laughing." I saw his hand grip the door-knob so tightly that the knuckles whitened. "Has she said anything about what happened?"

"Last night. . . ."

"I know about last night. I'm speaking of this morning."

I reminded myself that he had been through a great deal, that it was no wonder he chose to be abrupt. "Yes," I said. "She said that now that your—your father was dead she could eat her meals downstairs."

His shoulders stiffened. "And that seemed to please her?"

"Yes," I said. "It doesn't have to mean anything, does it? It's only natural. . . ."

"Nothing's natural," I heard him mutter. "Nothing that happens in this house is ever natural."

After he had gone, closing the connecting door behind him, I bathed in the adjoining bathroom, lying as long in the warm water as I dared, trying to relax, not thinking of what had occurred. I had nothing to wear except the full cotton skirt, the peasant blouse, and the sandals I had worn the day before, but I told myself that did not matter. If Paul wanted me to stay, I could return to the cottage for other clothes, or someone could be sent.

I stood in front of the mirror and combed my hair loose about my face and wondered whether I really wanted to stay. I had a choice. I owed no commitment to anyone at Pennarth—not even Paul. It was all very well to tell myself I wanted to help him because—because he was my friend, because he had saved me from sudden death, because the night before he had seemed to confide in me. But there was more to it than that. I had always been impulsive in the past, but this time impulse might mean that in the end I would be hurt.

Windows lined the stairs, and through them I could see that the fog had given way to a drizzling rain. The great hall was as ghostly as when I had first seen it. The dining room, however, was charming—not too large, with blue-

and-silver-striped paper coating the walls and blue-velvet drapes hiding the mist and rain outside.

Miranda was already sitting at the head of the long mahogany table wearing a tan sweater and skirt that were the most ordinary garments imaginable. There were even pearls around her neck, and her hair was caught back in a bun. I wondered if Paul had dictated her choice of clothes with an eye to the fact that today she would doubtlessly be interviewed by the police. She did not glance up as I came into the room but greedily concentrated on the food that piled her plate.

I joined Paul at a sideboard topped with silver chafing dishes. Without speaking he handed me a plate and took the top off each dish to allow me to choose from a lavish variety of scrambled eggs, sausages, bacon, hot porridge, kippers, and fried tomatoes.

"It was my father's desire that breakfasts be provided in the old-fashioned style," he murmured as I helped myself to eggs and bacon and waited while he poured tea into a delicate, broad-brimmed cup. "It is only one of a number of things that will be changed."

I did not find it odd that he should feel it necessary to apologize to me. He knew enough about my background now to realize that in all this I would see nothing but waste. It pleased me that he had bothered to explain.

We ate in silence. Only when she had wiped her plate clean with a piece of toast did Miranda seem to become aware of our presence. "Now," she said brightly, focusing her dark eyes on me with that intensity I found so disturbing, "we will take a walk outside."

"It's raining," Paul said evenly. "Perhaps Miss Grey—"

"Sara!" Miranda spat out my name. "Call her Sara!"

Paul ignored the outburst. "Besides," he said, "I'm afraid that before you do anything else, you will have to talk with the inspector." He glanced at his watch. "He should be here any minute now."

For the first time since I had come into the room,

Miranda looked at him directly. "Inspector?" she demanded. "I don't know any inspector."

Paul's face became expressionless. "He's in charge of
the police investigation of my father's death," he said. "It
is necessary that he interview everyone in this house."

"No!" She flared into a temper as suddenly as she had
done when Ron had tried to question her the night before.
She rose, pushing back her chair with so much violence
that it toppled to the floor. "No!" she repeated.

I looked at Paul. He nodded. I knew he wanted me to
do something, but what? I relied, as I had done before, on
intuition.

"Before you see anyone," I told her, "both of us must
have some more breakfast. Here. Bring your plate."

I had not expected her to be so easily diverted, but she
did as I said, actually smiling as I took the cover off one
chafing dish after another and measured out small portions
of everything for her. While her back was to the table, I
looked and saw Paul drop a pill, which he had taken from
a small vial, into her tea.

By the time we had returned to the table, the vial was
back in his pocket and her chair was in place. He held it
for her, and then both he and I returned to our seats. I did
not look at him. Pushing the eggs I did not really want
back and forth in my plate, I examined my own reaction
to the fact that he had undoubtedly given her some drug
that would calm her.

Something about the secretiveness of the act repelled
me. But what choice did he have? It meant only that he
wanted her to appear before the inspector in as normal a
state as possible, that he wanted her to give calm testimony about what had happened. She ate and drank. The
minutes seemed to drag. Was it my imagination, or were
her movements becoming perceptibly slower. Suddenly she
put her elbows on the table and propping her chin in her
hands, began to hum. Paul rose and went to the farther
side of the room and pushed back a drape. He pretended

to stare out into the drenched, mist-shrouded world out-side. I joined him. Miranda did not seem to notice.

"All right," he said when I was standing beside him. "We've got this far. Now, I'm going to see if I can arrange things so that you can go into the interview with her." His voice was so low that I had to come very close to him in order to hear. He put his hand on my arm. The fingers seemed to burn my skin. I felt strangely light-headed. It was all I could do to concentrate on what he was saying.

"The inspector realizes that my—my wife has very little emotional control," Paul went on. "And, of course, he knows that she found the body. I was able to convince him that anything she might have said to him last night would not be helpful. At first he wanted to make difficulties, but when his men returned from the cottage and told him about her condition, he agreed to wait. But it is vital that she give a coherent account of what happened as soon as possible. I think possibly this is more likely if you are with her, if she thinks that you, as well as she, are being questioned."

Perhaps because we were both so certain that Miranda was lost in her own drowsy thoughts, we had let our voices rise. At all events she heard us. Looking over Paul's shoulder, I saw that she had turned in her chair and was staring at us reflectively. At that moment anyone who did not know her would, I think, have been willing to swear that she was in perfect emotional control.

"You don't have to make plans, you know," she said. Her voice was clear and even. "I'm perfectly capable of talking to the police by myself."

"But a moment ago you said. . . ."

She rubbed her forehead. "I don't remember," she told him. "Besides, it doesn't matter what I said. I want to see the inspector alone."

I found myself moving toward her. "Are you quite cer-tain," I said, "that you wouldn't feel more comfortable if I were there?"

Her fingers pressed tighter against her forehead as though she were making a desperate attempt to think clearly. "No," she said. "There's a reason, you see. I thought of it a minute ago."

"A reason for what?"

"The man called Ron," she said heavily. "I want to tell them about Ron. And if you're with me, I won't be able to do that, will I? Because you promised not to tell."

Ten minutes later she was closeted with the inspector, a tall red-haired man who had arrived shaking the rain off his old-fashioned wide-brimmed derby and muttering imprecations against the weather. Paul met him in the great hall, took his coat, and ushered him into the den. Through the half-opened door I saw him introducing the policeman to Miranda, who was maintaining a fairly poised appearance, although her head seemed to be too heavy for her to hold completely straight. No matter what she intended to tell the inspector, I hoped that she would be able to keep from becoming too logy. The inspector might not be too happy if he realized she had been drugged before the interview.

When Paul emerged from the room, closing the door behind him, I was standing by one of the long windows of the great hall, staring out into a landscape twisted by the effect of the pouring rain against the glass. I could see the inspector's car by the front entrance and the back of the head of a man seated in the passenger seat. I assumed that it was one of the police officers who had come to the cottage the night before and wondered why he had not come inside. I heard Paul's feet on the parquet floor as he approached me through the shadows. When I turned to face him, I found myself looking into angry eyes.

"Why didn't you tell me?" he demanded in a low voice.

I stared at him, puzzled. "Tell you what?"

"Whatever it is that my wife intends to tell the inspector

about Ron Farrow. I take it that whatever it is, it's something you knew about."

I shrugged, startled by the hostility in his voice. "In the first place," I said, "I haven't had a chance to talk to you alone since I've come here. And in the second place it isn't that important."

"Why don't you let me decide that?"

His voice was gentler now, but I could see that he was making a conscious effort to keep it that way.

"It's only that when Miranda came to the cottage last night, Ron was there."

There was no reason why I should suddenly feel guilty, but I could feel my face grow hot. I turned back to stare out the window.

"Do you mean he came after I left?"

"He certainly wasn't there when you were, was he?" I snapped.

"Listen, Sara." He touched my shoulder. "I'm sorry. Look at me. You know I've been under considerable pressure. So much pressure that I haven't even thanked you for coming here. I quite honestly don't know how I would have managed things last night if you hadn't been with Miranda."

"It's all right," I said. "It's just that when you speak to me that way. . . ."

"I know," he said. The sadness on his narrow face might have been etched by the shadows, but I was looking directly into his dark eyes, and I could see the regret quite clearly in them.

"Tell me about Ron," he said. "Why did he come?"

For a moment I had to pause to remember. "He said—he said that ever since he'd talked to me at Bertha and Greg's, he hadn't been able to stop thinking about Eileen and what happened. He said that ever since she died, he'd been—well, incapable of thinking coherently about it. But then when he knew I was living at the cottage—they met at the cottage sometimes."

"I know," Paul muttered. "I know."

"Well, ever since he'd started thinking about me and the cottage, all of it had come back. He thought if he came there, he might be able to face what had happened. It was a sort of test. At first he couldn't make himself come inside. We sat on the doorstep and talked."

"What time was that?"

"A little past ten."

"How much after ten?" Paul demanded. "Don't you see, that's important."

For a moment I did not understand what he meant. Then I remembered Enoch telling me that Paul's father had been murdered at about ten. "But you don't think——"

"I know that despite what the police may believe, I didn't kill him," Paul said from between clenched teeth. "As far as I'm concerned, anyone who was on these grounds last night at about the time of his death is suspect."

"But what reason would Ron have to murder him?" I said. What Paul was suggesting made me feel as though someone had struck me.

"He had as much reason as any one of us," Paul replied. "But we can talk about that later. You're going to have to tell all this to the inspector. Miranda may have said that she was going to, but God knows how close to the truth anything that she will say may be. And before you talk to anyone else about this, I want to know about it."

"All right," I began reluctantly. I felt a sense of betrayal in telling Paul anything about Ron. "There really isn't much to tell. He asked me about my—my relationship with you. I mean, he saw you driving me out of St. Ives that afternoon after I talked to him. He wanted to know how I felt about you."

Suddenly Miranda's laughter rose, muted by the oak door that hid her from us but somehow incredibly penetrating. Paul's shoulders stiffened, and his face seemed to grow longer and narrower. Miranda laughed again, a shrill, hysterical laugh, and then there was silence.

"All right," Paul said, making an obvious effort to remember what I had been saying. "Have you any idea why he was asking questions about our—our relationship, as you put it?"

There was something incredibly cruel about the way he phrased the question. Or was it that I was being abnormally sensitive?

"He wanted to know if you had talked about him," I said. "About him and your sister."

"And did you tell him that we had talked about her?"

"No," I protested. "But somehow he seemed to know. I can remember thinking at one point—it was something he said—that he might have overheard us talking when we walked down to the cottage from here. It was so foggy. Anyone could have been quite close to us without our knowing. I don't mean that he might have deliberately followed us. You understand that, don't you?"

Paul stared past me reflectively. "I suppose he could have heard. But if he had, it would have meant that he'd been hanging about the estate from five until past ten when he came to see you."

"Not necessarily," I argued. "He used to live in the village, didn't he? He could have come to Pennarth for—for some reason and then changed his mind and started back, come across us in the mist, and overheard part of our conversation. He could have left the grounds after that and then decided to visit me."

"Did anything he said indicate that was the way it was?" Paul shot the question at me rapidly, as though there were not much time. And I knew that might well be true. At any moment Miranda might collapse into hysterics, and the interview would come to an end.

"I think he said that he had started off from St. Ives that morning and then turned back and later changed his mind." It was, I found, difficult for me to remember anything now except the way Ron had gripped my arm when I had tried to leave him and go inside the cottage.

"All right, what else did he say?"

"He asked me what your father had said to me that afternoon."

"How did he know that you'd been here to see him? Did you tell him that?"

"No. I asked him, and he said he had been guessing. I told him I wanted to go inside, that I didn't want to talk anymore."

"Why? Was he hostile?"

"He was pressing me," I said. "But surely that's understandable."

"Did you leave him then?"

"No. He—he wouldn't let me."

"He stopped you physically?" Paul's voice was harsh.

"He wouldn't help me get up. I couldn't stand on my ankle very well. He took my arm and held me."

Paul took a deep breath. His face was grim. "What else?" he demanded.

"He wanted to know if your father discussed Eileen with me."

"Why in God's name would he have done that?"

"I don't know. I couldn't make out what he was getting at. He—he frightened me. And then I was angry."

For a moment a smile touched Paul's lips. "You have a habit of getting angry, don't you? All right. I want you to tell the inspector everything about this, you understand. Don't keep anything back. Is there more?"

"He implied that you had followed me to St. Ives that day," I said slowly. "He said it wasn't any accident that you picked me up at the bus stop. He insisted that you had followed me to Greg and Bertha's, that you were aware I had met him there."

"And why was I supposed to have done that?" Paul's voice was scornful. Suddenly I found myself wishing that he had denied Ron's accusation.

"Because—this part wasn't clear. He said that your aunt had known that your sister's death wasn't an accident, that Enoch would have told her that, and that she left me the cottage with the understanding that I come here and—"

"Yes. Go on."

"That I come here and find out the truth. He said that she'd had her own life ruined by your father."

"He was implying, then, that my father was responsible for my sister's death?"

"He didn't put it just that way," I said. "But yes. Yes, I think that's what he meant."

Paul moved past me and traced an unseen picture on the glass of the window. The police car was still where I had seen it parked, and the man was still sitting in it. A fresh torrent of rain drowned the view, but Paul continued to stare out the window.

"And did you?" I heard him say.

"I don't know what you mean." But I did know. He was asking me if his aunt had left me the cottage on condition that I come here as some sort of spy. I was chilled by the thought that he would think me capable of it.

"I don't mean anything," he said roughly, turning to face me. His hands reached out and then fell to his sides. "And then, I suppose, Miranda made her arrival."

"Ron heard the ambulance pass," I said, conscious of an extraordinary sense of relief. "He went down to the main gate and found her there, trying to wrench it open. Apparently she thought the ambulance was going to come in that way."

"Who knows what she was thinking," Paul said in a low voice. "Who knows what she's saying in there now. But when she's done, you must talk to the inspector. Will you do that, Sara?"

"Yes," I murmured. "If you think it will help."

"I don't know whether it will help or not. But he must be told everything that might possibly be important about last night. One more thing. Miranda said she would have to tell him about Ron because you had promised——"

"I didn't promise anything," I told him. "Ron left the cottage by the back way when the police arrived to bring Miranda back here. He said he didn't want to talk to them then and warned me not to tell them that he had been there."

Paul's dark eyes narrowed. "What sort of threat did he make? He did threaten you, didn't he?"

"No," I said. "Not directly. He said that if I told them he had been there, he would tell them things about you that you didn't want known."

This time Paul's hands touched mine. "He couldn't tell them anything that would harm me," he said softly. "Do you believe me when I say that, Sara?"

There was no chance for me to answer. The door to the den was suddenly flung open, and Miranda appeared, her black hair no longer knotted neatly at the back of her head but hanging in its usual tangle around her face. During some stage in the interview she had apparently clutched at the pearls around her neck and broken the strand, because a string of them dangled from one hand, and pearls formed a tapping trail behind her as she hurried up the stairs.

The inspector moved toward us, his thick bony face wearing an odd expression which could have been one of bewilderment. "I think, Mr. Randolph," he said in a gruff voice, coming to a halt before Paul, "that you might wish to consult your solicitor before we proceed any further in this matter. The fact is, your wife has informed me that she was witness to the fact that you struck the fatal blow that killed your father."

5

"You can't possibly believe that!" I burst out.

The red-haired man gave me a curious glance. "I don't believe I've had the honor. . . ." he began.

"This is Inspector Devlon," Paul said in a low voice. "Miss Sara Grey. She is the present owner of the cottage at the foot of the estate."

"Ah, yes." The inspector fastened his brown eyes on me. He was a stocky figure clothed in a greenish tweed suit. He could just as well have been one of the local farmers dressed in his Sunday best except for the air of confidence he exuded. That and the boldness of his eyes. "Tell me, Miss Grey," he said, "have you any particular reason for thinking that Mrs. Randolph might have lied about this matter?"

I glanced at Paul. His face was white and set, his expression withdrawn. I thought it quite possible that he might not be hearing a word that was said.

"I was the first person to talk with her after she discovered the body," I said clearly. "She arrived at the cottage at a little before eleven. She was quite distraught, but she managed to tell me what had happened. And she said nothing—nothing—about having seen the murder committed."

The words had left my mouth before I remembered that they were not quite true. Miranda had said something about having seen someone. I closed my mind to the memory. She had said nothing about having witnessed Paul commit murder. And if she had, surely she would have said so.

"I will be glad to hear anything that you have to say on this subject, Miss Grey," the inspector told me. "Just at the moment I think you will agree with me, Mr. Randolph, that your solicitor should be consulted. You may prefer to have him with you before. . . ."

Inclining his head, Paul turned and started toward his den. "One other thing," the inspector called after him. "I have another person who wishes to give evidence outside in my car. He did not wish to come in until I had interviewed your wife."

Paul halted and looked back at us. "Who?" he said. "Who is it?"

"A Mr. Ron Farrow. I believe that you know of him. With your permission I will ask him to come inside."

"As you like."

Neither the inspector nor I spoke until the door to his den was closed behind him.

"Perhaps, Miss Grey," the police officer said, "you are acquainted with Mr. Farrow as well."

"If he's had any conversation with you at all," I said tight-lipped, "you must be aware of the fact that he visited my cottage on the night of the murder."

"It's interesting that you should choose to put it that way," the inspector said. "I would like to talk to both you and Mr. Farrow together. If you will excuse me for a moment, I will call him inside."

I followed him to the door. When he opened it, the rain pushed its way in with incredible force, soaking the parquet floor and the edge of the carpet. Ron had apparently been watching for a signal, for the door of the police car opened, and he appeared, the collar of his raincoat pulled high about his head. Once he was inside, it took all of the inspector's strength to push the door shut against the gale.

I do not think Ron had expected to find me there. He pushed away the long blond hair that was plastered wet over his high forehead and stared at me, not speaking. I turned away. I did not want any dialogue with him. In the confusion of my thoughts, it occurred to me that the most useful thing I could do at the moment was to talk to Miranda, to try to convince her that she had been wrong to lie about Paul. Or if not convince her, at least find out why she had wanted to do such a thing. I started up the stairs, and Ron pulled off his raincoat, his eyes following me.

"Miss Grey"—the inspector's voice was imperative—"I hope you won't mind if I request that you not leave us at this point. I particularly do not wish you to speak with Mrs. Randolph before we have had a chance to talk. In a very few minutes I'm sure that Mr. Randolph will have completed his telephone call, and the den will be available for our interview."

"I had no intention of speaking with Mrs. Randolph," I said stiffly. "I—I'm rather cold. I'd like to get a sweater from my room."

"By all means." The inspector smiled up at me with the self-satisfied expression of one who knows that he is in complete control of a particular situation. "By all means. Mr. Farrow and I will be waiting for you."

I turned and ran up the winding stairs, not quite knowing why I had lied about the sweater except that to have done otherwise would have been to let him guess that I had, in fact, intended to see Miranda. I had just reached the top of the stairs when I saw Enoch. He was standing in the doorway of Mr. Randolph's library, a hunched figure in the shadows.

"Enoch!" I exclaimed, hurrying toward him. "Listen. You must help me."

I spoke in a whisper, and yet he seemed to have no difficulty hearing me, although the night before he had claimed deafness when I mentioned Ron's name. There was, I thought, more to Enoch than the delightful old gentleman I had first taken him to be.

"Yes, my dear, what is it? As you see, I have been wandering about like a veritable ghost. Of no use, I fear, to anyone, although I will admit that I expected to be called into the inspector's presence before now."

"It's Miranda," I said. "The inspector talked to her this morning, and then she came dashing out of the den and ran upstairs."

"Yes, I saw her." The old man nodded his thatch of white hair at me. "She seemed to be upset, but that in itself is not unusual."

I took his hand. The flesh seemed strangely cold under my fingers. Outside the wind buffeted the window at the end of the hall. "Did she go to her room?" I demanded, casting a swift glance at the stairs. It was possible that the inspector might decide to follow me upstairs.

"Yes, she's in her room."

I was grateful to Enoch for not asking any unnecessary questions. He seemed to know that I had not much time.

"Do you suppose," I said, "that she would talk to you?"

The old man hunched his shoulders, his neck disappearing into them like a turtle's. He was wearing a black suit that fitted him loosely, as though the last time he had worn it he had been a bigger man. It flashed through my mind that he was the only one of us to make any display of mourning.

"Sometimes she treats me in quite a friendly fashion,"

he said. "I think I told you that when she wants to get away from the main part of the house, she often comes to me in my small sitting room. The elder Mr. Randolph looked with disapproval on such visits, naturally. He belonged to the old school in which one did not fraternize with servants. But, forgive me, my dear, I am rambling."

"The inspector doesn't want me to talk to Miranda," I whispered, "until he's talked to me first. At least that's what he says. I think actually he's afraid that I or someone may make her change her testimony—or statement, or whatever you want to call it."

It was, I found, harder to explain than I had imagined. "I don't know what else she told Devlon," I said, impatient with my own awkwardness, "but she *did* claim that she saw Paul kill his father."

Enoch drew in his breath, making a sound like that of a leaking bellows. "Did she, now?" he exclaimed. "Ah, the lady's a caution, no doubt about it. I don't suppose the inspector took her word as gospel."

"I think he's taking her quite seriously," I said. "But you and I know that she must be lying."

"You and I *hope* that she is lying," Enoch said carefully. "Or to be kinder, that she was simply confused when she said it. I take it that you want me to talk to her."

"Try to make her tell you who she really saw," I said. "If she saw anyone. Or find out why she said it."

"I can tell you that," Enoch said heavily. "She hates Paul because somehow, ten years ago, she got it into her mind that Paul helped to conspire to kill his sister. Miranda doted on Eileen. Ah, it's all been a sad story, my dear."

What he had said took me so completely by surprise that I could not make an answer nor ask a question. My mind seemed to be flying off in all directions. I knew only that I had to go back downstairs if I did not want the inspector to think I had gone to Miranda.

"Talk to her," I whispered to Enoch. "Make her see reason."

I literally ran to my room and grabbed a sweater from my overnight case, not bothering to notice whether the connecting door to Miranda's room was open or not. When I came out into the hall again, Enoch had disappeared. I prayed that he was with her. She could do so much harm if what he said were true. But it seemed inconceivable that she could blame Paul for what had happened to Eileen.

Hurrying down the stairs, I found Paul just emerging from the den. His face was white and drawn. "My solicitor —an old friend—has agreed to come down from London today," he said. "I explained the situation to him in some detail."

"*Your* account of the situation," Ron muttered. "For God's sake, let's be accurate while we still can be. Before a convocation of expensive lawyers gets to work on this."

I was standing on the third step from the bottom of the stairs, and in the same moment that Ron spoke I caught a glimpse of someone moving in the part of the hall adjacent to the green-baize door that led to the servants' quarters. From my position above the others I could just make out, through the gloom, the thin figure of the housekeeper as she stood listening.

"I think perhaps that Mrs. Herrick wants something," I said loudly.

The woman started and shrank back toward the door. Paul turned his head and called to her. I could not tell from the sound of his voice whether he realized I had been telling him that the woman had been eavesdropping.

As Grace Herrick moved reluctantly out of the shadows, Paul turned back to the inspector. "If you don't mind," he said, "I'm going to send Mrs. Herrick up to my wife. When she's upset, it's often not wise to leave her alone."

The inspector glanced at me and then at Paul, obviously

deliberating the question. Ron kept his eyes on the thin figure of the woman who was slowly making her way toward them. I wondered if the two knew one another. Was she from the village originally? But that did not matter. What mattered was that Paul be kept from sending her up to Miranda to destroy whatever contact Enoch had managed to make with her. The inspector's back was now toward me. I made a movement with my hand, and when Paul looked up, I shook my head and mouthed Enoch's name.

"On the other hand," he said, apparently catching my meaning immediately, "it might be just as well, under these circumstances, that she be left to herself. Is the back door bolted, Mrs. Herrick?"

The housekeeper's tight dark face was expressionless. "Yes," she said.

"Fine. I would like you to remain in the kitchen with the door opened so that if my wife comes downstairs, you can let me know. The weather isn't fit for her to be wandering outside."

The housekeeper inclined her head. "Is that all, sir?" she asked. Perhaps it was my imagination, but I seemed to hear a mocking note in her voice.

"Yes, that's all," Paul said impatiently. "These precautions may seem a bit extreme to you, Inspector, but I assure you they are necessary. Miss Grey will testify to that."

"I imagine," Ron said, his eyes still on Grace Herrick as she made her way toward the green-baize doors, "that Miss Grey will testify to a good many things before all of this is over."

Paul ignored him. He did not betray any reaction at all to the fact that Ron was here. And that was strange. Unless he had expected that the younger man's desire to implicate him in his father's death would draw him here.

"Would you like to talk to any one of us alone, Inspector?" he said. "If so, my den is at your disposal."

"I think," the inspector said slowly, "I would like to talk to all three of you. Yes, that procedure would suit me best. There are very few things left to clear up."

It was not clear to me whether he meant to imply that Paul was about to be charged with murder or not, but Ron apparently interpreted it to mean that, for he smiled as he and I followed the inspector into the den. Paul joined us after locking the front door, and I knew that he was still thinking of Miranda and the possibility that she might try to leave the house. After the trouble she had apparently determined to cause him, I wondered that he could still care one way or another about her safety.

Paul's den was small and, surprisingly in this house, low-ceilinged, perhaps because a good part of it seemed to run under the main stairway. The only windows were small and mullioned, set to the right of the center of the wall faced as one came through the door, and giving a view of nothing except the stone wall of the crumbling tower, now half hidden by the slashing rain. It seemed quite possible that the door to the left of the same wall must lead directly to the tower. The walls of the room were paneled in oak, and the floor was covered with a thick green rug which absorbed the sound of our footsteps.

We stood in silence listening to the rain beat against the windows until Paul joined us. Then the inspector, with a nod which might have indicated an apology for usurping Paul's position, took a seat behind the long oak desk. Glancing over my shoulder as I took the chair that Paul drew up to the desk for me, I saw that the wall behind me was lined solidly with books and that the door had been left open, probably to enable him to hear Miranda if she came down the stairs. I thought that was unwise, because it was quite possible the housekeeper might return to eavesdrop, despite his orders that she remain in the kitchen.

"Very well, then," Inspector Devlon said, smoothing back his red hair with one hamlike hand. "Now, I recognize that it is difficult to create any particular sympathy for my position. I see you, for example, Miss Grey, glaring at me as though I were your mortal enemy, even though we met for the first time minutes ago. As for Mr. Farrow," he turned to Ron, "you came here, as I well recognize, not to assist me in my work, but to satisfy your own desire for revenge.

"There's no need to protest. That is as good a reason for giving evidence against another man as any. As for you, Mr. Randolph, your position is, perhaps, even more difficult than mine. You have not made a point of this fact to me, but I well recognize that your wife's testimony may never be taken into account by any court. You must have reason to question my haste in bringing a charge."

He took out a pipe with a huge protruding bowl and proceeded to pack it with tobacco. Everything about him, including the speech he was now in the process of delivering, seemed to reflect a plodding quality which irritated me beyond measure. I glanced at Paul, but he was apparently intent on listening to Devlon, while Ron, in the chair beside him, stared at the floor. Beside Paul he looked almost deliberately shabby in paint-stained slacks and a sweater that had come unraveled at the sleeves.

"I only wish to make this point clear," the inspector went on. "All acts of murder are committed by those who have means, motive, and opportunity. It is my function to determine on one person, or, in the event of conspiracy, a group of persons, who can, under these three conditions, appropriately be charged."

He brought the pipe to his lips and lighting a match, laboriously proceeded to light it. Ron began to beat a tattoo on the floor with the heel of one shoe, and I found myself shifting restlessly in my chair. It was no surprise to me that this man had driven Miranda to hysterics. After a few minutes of exposure to him, she probably felt driven to say anything that came into her mind in order to be released from his presence.

"Now," the inspector said, the bovine brown eyes surveying us from beyond a pall of smoke, "the means were readily available to anyone who came inside this house. The hammer with which Mr. Randolph was killed has been identified by the housekeeper as one that was kept in the tool cupboard in the back hall. The next step was to determine who was in this house at about the hour of ten last night, and we have, by their own admission, six persons, at least, who fall into this category. It was quite proper that all should be here.

"Unfortunately only two of these people—the maids—can give evidence as to one another's activities during the time in question. But that need not concern us at the moment. This is an isolated estate, but it is possible that someone else besides these six persons was in the house. Therefore, before I take what would appear to be the next obvious step, I must satisfy myself that those other people who were in the vicinity of Pennarth last night were not, in fact, inside the house itself. You, for example, Miss Grey? Where were you at the time in question?"

He shot out the question with a sudden departure from his leisurely progress, pointing the stem of his pipe at me as though it were an accusing finger.

"At ten?"

"Let us say from nine thirty until ten."

"I was inside my cottage."

"Ah. Can this be verified by any other person?"

I turned reluctantly to Ron. "Mr. Farrow appeared at my door at ten or a little after," I said. "He knows I was there."

"You speak of Mr. Farrow formally. Is he a friend of yours?"

"Not a friend," I said clearly. "We had met once before at the home of mutual acquaintances in St. Ives."

"Under those conditions it would seem that ten o'clock at night would be a rather strange time for a casual acquaintance to make a call," the inspector reflected. "But we will consider that later. Where had Mr. Farrow been before he appeared at your cottage?"

"Listen," Ron said, pushing back his chair and rising. "I agreed to come here because you damn well made it appear that this is the only place you would listen to me. But it's no good your trying to involve me in whatever happened here. If you want to hear what I have to say, let's get to it without all this rigamarole."

"Sit down, Mr. Farrow," the inspector said calmly. "I'm afraid that you will have to follow whatever procedure I care to adopt. You may have volunteered your testimony, but I assure you that once Miss Grey told us you were at her cottage last night—actually on the estate—you would have been questioned whether you wanted to be or not."

He turned to me, sucking on the huge pipe, his cheeks scarlet with the effort. Under other circumstances I might have found him amusing. Now I saw in him only a threat to Paul. He had apparently made it obvious to Paul, even before Miranda's testimony, that he was suspect. I saw in him the sort of man who would go plodding on to a previously established goal no matter what happened. Ron might feel himself threatened, but I knew better. All that Devlon was intent on doing now was finding a few more details that would conclude his case against Paul or, at least, give him enough proof to make a legitimate charge.

"Now, if we may, Miss Grey," the inspector said briskly. "Where did Mr. Farrow say that he had been before he arrived at your cottage at about ten?"

"He could have told me anything," I reminded him. "Actually, he didn't say. He mentioned starting out for Pennarth that morning from St. Ives and changing his mind. Then, apparently, he changed it again. But I don't know when. He could have just arrived on the estate, or he could have been here for hours."

"I'm going to add something to that, Devlon," Ron said belligerently. "You ought to understand that Miss Grey, as you call her, will do anything she can to make it appear that I might have been involved in this murder."

"I can't say, Mr. Farrow, that I have seen any indication on her part to implicate you."

"Can't you? I should say it was perfectly clear that she's just implied that I could have been on the estate, or in this house, for that matter, at the time that the murder was committed."

"And were you, Mr. Farrow?"

For the second time that morning I was aware that the inspector was a shrewder man than one might be tempted to give him credit for being. Without any apparent effort he had managed to jockey Ron into admitting that it was quite possible that he, too, could have had what the inspector liked to term "opportunity."

"No!" Ron seemed to explode. His long face was white, and his youth disappeared in the twisting of his facial muscles. "No! I was not on the grounds of this lousy estate, or in this house, either. I left St. Ives at about eight thirty and finally got a ride."

"You hitchhiked?"

"Yes, dammit, I hitchhiked. We all can't afford powerful sports cars. They let me off at the road that forks west just beyond the village, and I walked the rest of the way."

"Who let you off?"

"Some old character in a beat-up Austin. How the hell should I know who he was?"

"How, indeed?" The inspector made a great business of knocking out his pipe in a glass ashtray. "No doubt if your story needs to be verified, we can locate the 'old character,' as you call him. All right, then. Now we have your word as to your whereabouts, Mr. Farrow, during the vital time —which is no more nor less than what we have from most of the other—er—principals involved. What about you, Miss Grey?"

"If you mean, where was I at the time the murder was committed," I snapped, "I've already told you I was at the cottage."

"Now, that's not precisely what you said," the inspector declared in a teasing voice, which made me want to scream with sheer annoyance. "You said you were there when Mr. Farrow arrived."

"I can testify that it was not possible for Miss Grey to have been anywhere else before that time," Paul said in a low voice. "I was with her, as you know, until after seven. She had hurt her ankle by falling against a rock when we came back to the cottage from this house earlier in the afternoon. When I left her, her ankle was still paining her considerably. She was in no condition to have come here to the house, killed my father, and gotten back at her home in time to open the door for Mr. Farrow at ten."

The sarcasm in his voice seemed to be lost on the inspector, who beamed and half rose in his chair to peer over the desk at my leg. "Yes, yes," he said delightedly, "I seem to see a bit of swelling. I assume, Miss Grey, that you would not protest if we had a doctor verify that you did, in fact, do a damage to your leg. It falls in the same category, we might say, of finding the old character who gave Mr. Farrow a ride. A precautionary verification and quite essential, perhaps, in view of the fact that just a few minutes ago I saw you run up the stairs with little apparent effort." He lowered himself back into his chair and let his brown eyes rest on me reflectively.

"Last night it ached a good deal," I said coldly. "Mr. Farrow could, if he wished, verify the fact that I could scarcely stand without support."

Ron glared at me. "What in hell is all this Mr. Farrow stuff?" he demanded. "Yes, you did appear to be in considerable pain when you tried to stand. You *appeared* to be. That's all I can say, since, unlike Mr. Randolph, I wasn't privileged to be on hand when the accident occurred."

"Ah, that's very helpful, Mr. Farrow. Very helpful. We can assume, then, that unless Miss Grey was doing a very effective job of acting—and, of course, we all know that women, by their very natures, are quite capable of being excellent actresses—she can be eliminated from our list of—er—suspects."

"I doubt very much," Paul said sarcastically, "that Miss Grey would be capable, even if she had been able physically, of beating in the head of an old man with a hammer for no reason whatsoever."

The inspector demonstrated interest by twitching his thick features upward until his eyebrows met his fringe of red hair. "But I understood that Miss Grey knew your father—had, in fact, an appointment with him the afternoon before his death."

"I explained all that when I told you that I accompanied her back to the cottage," Paul said in a flat voice.

The inspector kept his brown eyes on me. "And was the interview a pleasant one, Miss Grey?" he said.

Ron sneered his amusement at me.

"Not particularly," I responded.

"Perhaps you would like to tell me why."

"He wanted me to give up the cottage," I said. "He did not like the idea of having a stranger living on the estate."

"That's fine," the inspector chortled. "I mean to say that it's very refreshing to encounter such directness, Miss Grey. Perhaps you won't mind telling me what your response was."

"I said that I intended to remain on in the cottage."

"And was he pleased with your response?"

"No," I said. "In fact, he was considerably upset. But there was nothing that he could do."

"Nothing, Miss Grey? Mr. Randolph was, I understand, a very powerful man."

"The cottage is legally mine," I said. "His sister left it to me."

"Ah, but there are always ways, aren't there, Miss Grey? Established wealth has its ways."

"I don't know about that," I said. "I can only tell you that my only response to Mr. Randolph was to feel sorry for him. I certainly had no desire to see him dead."

"So he made no threats?"

"No," I said.

"And have you a witness to that?"

"No."

The inspector made a broad gesture with his farmer's hands. "So much," he mourned, "so very much will have to be taken on faith in this case. And let me assure you, my friend, that it is not wise to take anything on faith when murder is involved."

He paused, looking at each of us in turn with what I assumed he meant to be dramatic deliberation. "I can think of no further questions to ask," he said. Behind him the rain beat a steady pulse against the window. It might have been evening for all the light that streamed in from outside.

"Then perhaps we can get to me," Ron said impatiently. "I don't know why you wanted me to come out here, anyway. I could have said what I had to say just as well in your office in town."

"I realize, Mr. Farrow, that was what you had in mind," the inspector said calmly. "However, since what you had to say was in the nature of a direct charge against Mr. Randolph here, I thought it would be advisable for him to hear you give evidence against him. That was, of course, before I talked to Mrs. Randolph. It is not often that anyone voluntarily gives evidence in a murder case, and I wanted to—what shall I say?—take maximum advantage of the situation."

I glanced at Ron. He had warned me, when he left the cottage the night before, that he could, if he wished, do Paul some harm. Instinctively, I had believed him capable of anything. That was why, after that one slip, I had not mentioned even to Enoch that he had been with me. Yet without any evidence that I had disclosed his presence at the cottage, he had gone to the police. I guessed from the expression on his face that he had gone with information that he had expected to impart to them alone. I was glad, at least, that the inspector had arranged matters so that Paul could, if he wished, defend himself. But I was not certain that had been Devlon's actual motive for bringing him here. At this point, in fact, I realized that I was certain about nothing.

Ron was standing now, and there was a dignity about him, despite the shabbiness of his clothes. There was certainly nothing boyish about the way he spoke. Even his insolence had disappeared.

"There's been a mistake," he said. "On your part, Inspector. I don't know what I might have said that would have prompted you to think that I came to you to give evidence against Mr. Randolph." He paused to glance at Paul. The contrast between the two men had never been more apparent. Paul, the shadows throwing his high cheekbones into relief, was the more ominous in appearance. And yet it was Ron I feared.

"If I had any such evidence, I would give it with the greatest pleasure," Ron went on. "But I wasn't here last night. I didn't see anything that could have pertained to the murder. It's obvious that an only son of a wealthy man probably stands to profit by his father's death. I mean, if you're interested in motives, that's only one of a number I could name. But the reason I came to your office, Inspector, was because I was fairly certain that Sara here would have told you that I was on the estate last night, and it occurred to me that she might try to use me as a red herring.

"She might try to divert your interest in the younger Mr. Randolph by hinting that it was possible I had something to do with his father's death. The only reason I came to you, Devlon, was because I wanted to protect myself. When you suggested that I come along out here with you, I was certain someone was trying to involve me. So I was willing to come and defend myself. But now I see there's no need of that. Everything I intended to say has been said. I was at Sara's cottage at ten last night. She says a little after ten. I would have said a little before. I came directly from St. Ives. At no time was I at this house. And now, Inspector, if you have any more business here, I think I'll wait in the car."

The policeman eyed Ron reflectively, sucking on his now cold pipe. "Yes, sir," he said as Ron reached the door. "Why don't you do that?"

Perhaps Ron expected to be urged to stay. At any rate, he turned, his hand on the knob, and stared at the inspector. "Is that all you have to say after driving me all the way out here?" he demanded angrily.

"That appears to be about all you're willing to let me say," the inspector suggested. "Actually, I'm not at all convinced that you did come to my office this morning simply to 'cover yourself.' I think you came for quite another reason, but something you've heard or seen since we came here to Pennarth has induced you to change your mind about any particular confidences you had planned to make in me."

Ron started to protest, but the inspector silenced him by raising his broad hand, palm outward. "Now, as for why I brought you out here," he said, "I've already explained that to my own satisfaction, if not to yours. If you'd said what you intended to say, Mr. Randolph here could have defended himself. And something might have come out of it. As it is, I expect that I'll have to stick to my original decision. I'm afraid, Mr. Randolph, that I must ask you to come back to town with me."

The housekeeper folded her hands under her white apron in a manner that I thought was deliberately servile. Everything about her seemed to proclaim the ideal servant, from the neatness of her black dress to the responsible, strong features of her face.

I had found her in the kitchen, polishing the bottom of a copper pan with the attitude of a woman who, in the absence of other duties, manufactures some. One of the

maids was busy at the sink, a huge iron affair that, with its
sideboard, stretched the length of one wall. It was the first
time I had seen any of the other servants, and the girl, an
unattractive, rather overweight blonde, eyed me with open
curiosity as Mrs. Herrick, her face expressionless, put
down the pan and came to the doorway to talk to me.

I explained that Mr. Randolph was expecting a call
from his solicitor when his train reached Truro. "It was
originally arranged that a car would be sent for him," I
said. "Now Mr. Randolph wants him to be told to go
directly to the police office in Truro, where Mr. Randolph
will meet him. Is that clear?"

"Quite clear, miss. May I ask how many people will be
here for lunch?"

Without any particular inflection of her voice she made
it clear that she disliked having to ask me anything that
had to do with household details. I was a stranger, and she
had seemed to find that offensive from the first moment
she had set eyes on me the afternoon before.

Although I could sympathize with her position, there
was something about the woman I mistrusted and disliked.
I remembered the stillness with which she had stood in the
shadows by the green-baize door, deliberately listening to
what was being said in the great hall. And I remembered,
too, the way her eyes had fastened on Ron as she had
come toward us. I wondered if the inspector had interviewed her the night before and what she had told him.
Had she, as well as Miranda, added credence to his belief
that Paul had murdered his father?

"Mrs. Randolph and I will be here," I said. "Mr. Randolph asked me to stay until he returned."

That was true enough. Standing a little apart from the
inspector and Ron, he had pulled on his raincoat and
made the request wearily. "I don't know what to expect,"
he had said, "but I'd be grateful if you would keep Miranda company. If, for some reason, I'm not able to return
to Pennarth tonight, my solicitor will call you."

The inference had been that he would not be able to call

himself. That meant he was fairly certain that he would be charged, but he said nothing of that possibility. Nor did I. I could not believe that he could be charged on the strength of Miranda's statement. If it had been anyone else, perhaps. But surely Devlon must have realized that she was all too capable of irrationality. It was incomprehensible that he would make a formal accusation unless what Miranda had told him had been verified by someone else.

"And dinner," Mrs. Herrick said stiffly. "Will Mr. Randolph be here for dinner?"

It was not the preparation of meals that she was really interested in. I knew that. Perhaps it was simple curiosity, but somehow I thought there was more to it than that.

"I'm not certain," I said, starting to turn away.

Her voice arrested me, and when I turned back, I saw that her face was no longer expressionless but twisted with emotion.

"And is it all right for the maids to proceed with their usual work?" she demanded.

"I imagine that it is," I said. "Unless the inspector indicated to you that he did not want certain rooms touched."

"He said naught to me," she replied, slipping for a moment into the local dialect, and I could see that beneath the apron she was clenching and unclenching her hands. "Things at sixes and sevens," she muttered. "And the funeral. What about that?"

She drew herself up to her full height. She was a taller woman than I had taken her to be—as tall as Miranda. In fact, in an odd way, there was a great similarity between their appearances. Both were dark. Mrs. Herrick was not as haggard as Miranda, yet I guessed that she was a few years older. In her fifties, perhaps. I had never imagined that she would lose control of herself, and I sensed that now she was very close to doing that. I moved into the hall, away from the curious stare of the maid, and she followed me, still, apparently, waiting for an answer to her question.

"I don't know anything about the funeral," I said in a

low voice. "Under the circumstances it may be delayed. But I wouldn't be concerned if I were you. Mr. Randolph will see to arranging everything. Things should be back to normal soon."

"Not if they try him for murder, they won't be," the housekeeper hissed. "Even if he does come back, things won't be the same. If anyone thinks I'm going to live in the same house where a murder's been committed, they're mistaken."

Much as I disliked and mistrusted the woman, the thought that she might pack her bags and leave the house to take care of itself appalled me. The realization that until Paul returned I seemed to be the person left in charge of Pennarth suddenly swept over me. It was a responsibility I did not want to assume.

"Mr. Randolph will be back," I said quietly, with a conviction I did not feel.

"With his wife telling everyone he killed his father." Mrs. Herrick's voice was scornful. "Not likely."

I stared at her, puzzled. As far as I could tell, she had no way of knowing what Miranda had said to the inspector. And then my gaze fell on the back stairs that led up into the shadows of the upper floor, and it occurred to me that when Paul had sent her back here to see that Miranda did not leave the house, she might have gone instead up to the bedroom where Enoch was closeted with her. She was, I knew, quite capable of eavesdropping. Perhaps she had heard Miranda telling Enoch what she had told the inspector.

"Finding her father-in-law's body was an upsetting experience for Mrs. Randolph," I said flatly. "At the moment I'm not at all certain that she knows what she's saying."

"Has she ever known?" the housekeeper demanded sotto voce with a glance back over her thin shoulder to the kitchen. "Or cared, for that matter. It's all very well for everyone around here to say that she's emotionally upset, whatever that means. If she's crazy, she ought to be locked up. That's what the elder Mr. Randolph said. He wouldn't let her in his sight, and now the moment he's gone and can't keep things under control, she tries to make trouble for her own husband. If anyone should have been murdered, it was her."

I did not have the vaguest idea what to say. The transformation from sphinx to fishwife had taken me too much by surprise.

"I'll tell you another thing," the housekeeper muttered, moving closer to me, her hands still working against one another under the apron. "If you're smart, you'll go back to your own place. That's what all of us ought to do. I've got a sister in the village who would take me in. We ought to leave her here alone so as she can't hurt anyone else. Murdered in our beds we'll be if we stay."

She seemed to be suggesting that Miranda had killed her father-in-law, but I could not be certain, and for some reason I did not want to ask her outright. All I was sure of was that I had made some sort of commitment to Paul to keep things from falling apart here.

"If you know anything you haven't told the police," I said in a low voice, "you ought to inform the inspector. As far as anyone else being murdered is concerned——"

A crash cut off my words. Involuntarily I started for the stairs.

"It came from outside," Mrs. Herrick said. "The next thing, this house will be falling in around our ears. I'm not staying here to be killed. I—"

I took her by the arm and pulled her to the arched door set deep in the thick walls. "Open it," I said, pointing to the massive old-fashioned bolt.

For a moment I thought she was going to protest. Then, wrenching her arm from my grasp, she took a key from the deep pocket of her apron and fitted it in the lock and pulled back the bolt. Opening the door, I stared out into rain that dashed against the house with such fury that I could not see more than two feet ahead of me. A broad

border of gravel appeared to line the house at the back. I
stepped out into the downpour, the wind catching my full
skirt and blowing it up over my face. Wrenching it down,
I saw in front of me a huge piece of slate, its edge penetrating the gravel like a knife. The wind seemed to be
carrying me back into the house, and it was only with
some effort that I closed the thick oak door against it.

"It's nothing," I gasped, wiping the moisture off my
face. "Only some slate from the roof. One thing's certain.
You'll never be able to make it to the village through
that." I pulled back my streaming hair from my face and
stared directly into the housekeeper's eyes. "The only thing
we can do is wait," I said. "Wait until the storm is over.
Wait for Mr. Randolph to come back."

Her eyes wavered. Without speaking she relocked the
door and bolted it. Glancing toward the kitchen, I saw the
maid cowering against the doorjamb, a terrified expression
on her plump face. "It's all right," I repeated. "It's only
some fallen slate from the roof."

I left them staring after me and hurried up the back
stairs. At the top of the stairs I met the other maid, hurrying along the passageway, a pile of sheets in her arms.
Repeating my reassurance, I passed her and hurried into
my bedroom. The next thing was to talk to Enoch and
Miranda, but first I had to change out of my wet clothes.

At the same moment that I remembered I had no
clothes to change into I saw what was spread out on the
bed. There was the wispy gray nightgown that Miranda
had brought into my room this morning, and neatly arranged beside it were skirts, dresses, sweaters, and blouses:
Eileen's clothes—the possessions of a girl who had died
ten years before. Miranda had said she had saved the
wardrobe. Obviously she had determined that I should
have them.

I hesitated. If Paul had been in the house, if there had
been any chance he might see me, I would not have considered wearing anything of his sister's. But he was not

here, and by the time he returned my own clothes would probably be dry. Meanwhile, there were things to be done.

I pulled off my wet things and hung them on hangers over the tub in the adjoining bathroom. Then I chose a brown tweed skirt and a blue sweater and put them on.

Paul's sister must have been exactly my size, for the garments fitted me perfectly. They were expensive clothes, the skirt lined with silk and the sweater a soft cashmere, the sort of clothes that time does not outdate. I turned and looked at myself in the mirror and for a moment, seemed to see a stranger there.

It was not simply that I was not accustomed to seeing myself in clothes as well cut as these. There was something about my hair, my eyes. . . . I wrenched myself away from such imaginings. The room was too shadowy, reflecting the pearly gray light from the rain and fog outside. In this light one might see ghosts anywhere.

Going to each window in turn, I pulled the brown drapes shut against the storm and switched on all the lights. Back at the mirror, I brushed my hair until it was nearly dry and twisted it in a single long braid at the back. A touch of color to my cheeks, and it was done. I was myself again, recognizable, complete. Then I hurried across the long room and opened the door to Miranda's bedroom.

I had assumed, since she was quiet, that Enoch had succeeded in calming her. The moment I saw her cowering in the far corner of the room I knew she was in a more disturbed state than I had ever seen her. She was still wearing the matronly skirt and sweater that Paul had chosen for her interview with the inspector. The broken strand of pearls that she had clutched as she ran out of the den had been tied back around her neck, half the pearls gone, the thread on which they were strung showing. Her dark hair had been pulled down about her face in limp strands, and she had taken off her shoes.

There was something more disheveled about her now

than there ever had been before, even when she had worn
the loose scarlet robe the night before. Enoch was sitting
in an armchair near the bed, his gnarled fingers pressed
against his forehead, his back bent so that I could see only
the crop of thick white hair. He looked up as Miranda
suddenly ran toward me, her arms outstretched.

"Eileen!" she cried. "You've come back! I always knew
you'd come back!"

She embraced me, crushing my face against her shoulder. With an effort I pulled myself away and stared helplessly at Enoch, who shook his head. Meaning what? That
I should not correct her? That he had been able to make
no progress in his talk with her? Perhaps both. All the life,
all the spirit, seemed to be drained from his face. He
looked incredibly old and totally exhausted.

Now Miranda was holding me at arm's length, her face
twisted into a grimace which caricatured happiness. "They
tried to tell me you were dead," she said in a shrill voice.
"Ever so long ago. But I knew it wasn't true. They sent
you away, didn't they? Like they did the time before. But
it's all right now. Now that he's dead, you can stay here
for as long as you like. You can stay here forever."

For a moment I was too startled to speak. Slowly the
delight faded from her face. "You *are* Eileen, aren't you?"
she demanded. She raised her arms, and lifting what was
left of the pearl necklace above her head, she brought it
down over mine and gripping it tight in one clenched fist,
tightened it until the exposed catgut bit into my skin. My
back was to Enoch, and I knew that he could not see what
was happening. Her strength was amazing. She twisted the
loop of pearls once more, and I felt myself begin to grow
dizzy. She was still talking, but I could scarcely hear the
words.

"You *are* Eileen, aren't you?" she muttered. "Because if
you aren't, then you're that woman Sara. She's Paul's
woman, you know. She sleeps in his bed. And she dresses
in your clothes. If it isn't you, Eileen, it's her. And I would
be very angry if it's her."

I reached up, gasping for breath, and tore at the gut, pulling it away from my neck. It broke, and what was left of the pearls scattered to the floor.

"Yes," I whispered, rubbing my neck. "Yes, I'm Eileen. I—I've come back, Miranda."

She smiled with the delight of a child, and I turned to Enoch. "Has she been like this long?" I asked in a low voice.

"I found her trying to unlock one of her bureau drawers," he murmured. "But the key—the key was broken. She was hysterical. Wanted me to open it. I managed to break the lock, and she started to pull out clothes. Eileen's clothes. I haven't been able to get her to talk about anything but Eileen coming back. And then you come in wearing——"

"No secrets!" Miranda cried gaily, whirling herself into the center of the room. "No more secrets ever. We have to celebrate. Someone must tell Paul that you're back. He'll be so glad."

"Paul's not here," I said. At least I could try to find out if she had any recollection of what had happened this morning. "He's gone off with the inspector."

"Inspector?" She laughed, flinging her long hair back over her shoulders. "I don't know any inspector."

"The policeman," I said slowly. "The man you talked to after breakfast. Remember? You told him that Paul had killed his father."

I had no idea what her reaction would be, but I had not expected laughter. She flung herself down on the floor and laughed, hugging herself.

"We're going to have to get her to quiet down," I said in a low voice to Enoch. "Paul gave her some sort of tranquilizer this morning. And Mrs. Herrick brought her a pill with her hot milk last night."

"I don't know anything about her medication," Enoch muttered under the sound of laughter which rose and fell rhythmically. "Perhaps Mrs. Herrick. . . ."

I pushed the bell beside the bed and then went to kneel

on the floor beside the hysterical woman. "Miranda!" I said, taking her by the shoulders and shaking her. "Come. Help me to pick up the pearls," I said, trying to keep my voice calm. "It's such a pretty necklace."

"Would you like it?" She stared at me eagerly. "Paul gave it to me, you know. I don't like pearls, but he gave them to me. He made me wear them this morning." She rubbed her forehead. "I can't remember why, but he made me wear them. He won't like it if he knows I've broken them."

I had managed to distract her. On her hands and knees she began to crawl around the floor, uttering little cries of pleasure each time she found one of the pearls. A knock sounded on the door. Getting to my feet, I hurried to open it. Miranda did not seem to notice.

"Another one!" she cried delightedly. "I've found another one!"

When I opened the door, Mrs. Herrick's eyes brushed past me and fastened on Miranda as she crawled about the floor. "The pills that you sent up with the milk last night," I said in a whisper. "They're to make her sleep?"

"That's what I was told, miss." The housekeeper kept her incredulous eyes on Miranda.

"Then have one brought up now," I said. "No, two. And some hot milk. As quickly as you can!"

She was back with a tray before Miranda had found the last pearl. Meanwhile, I had managed to tell Enoch what I intended to do—draw the curtains as though it were night and lay out a nightgown. I was amazed that the ruse worked as well as it did. Apparently completely unaware of Enoch's presence in the chair by the bed, Miranda undressed, put on the nightgown, took the two pills without question, drank the milk, and let me tuck her in.

"You won't go away again, will you, dear?" she said as I bent over her. "In the morning we'll go down to the cottage. We won't have to worry about that boy being there now. He doesn't come there anymore. No one comes there. We can go down to the cove and swim if it's warm." She clutched my hand. "Everything's going to be all right now, isn't it?" she demanded with something like desperation in her voice.

"Yes," I said. "Everything's going to be all right."

She fell asleep almost immediately. As soon as she was breathing deeply and evenly, I nodded reassuringly to Enoch and hurried out of the room and down the stairs to the great hall. One of the maids was dusting there. She stared after me curiously as I went into Paul's den and shut the door.

The telephone was on the desk. Paul had to be contacted. He would tell me what to do, what doctor to call. I had coped for the moment, but it was quite obvious that Miranda needed professional help at once. And the inspector had to be informed about her breakdown. Then, surely, he would realize that no charge she had brought against Paul could be seriously considered as evidence. I picked up the receiver and brought it to my ear. The line was dead.

In that same moment I heard the creaking of the door that led into the great hall. I ran out and saw three men. One of them, Ron, was leaning against the door, forcing it shut against the wind. The second man was being supported by the third. It was Paul, hurt. As I ran toward him, I saw the line of blood that streaked his face. The man supporting him was wearing the sort of long green slicker that fishermen wore. He turned, and I recognized Ora Johnson, the handyman who had taken care of the cottage for Miss Randolph.

"What's happened?" I demanded. "Paul, are you all right?"

He shook his head as though he were dazed and raised his hand to his forehead as though to try to staunch the blood. His raincoat was matted with mud.

"The estuary's flooded," Ora Johnson muttered. "Bridge

out. Whoever was driving didn't see that in time, I reckon."

"Where's the inspector?" I cried.

"Where do you think?" Ron was leaning back against the door, water streaming down over his face. "With any luck he's halfway out to open sea by now."

6

The fact that the inspector had drowned didn't really register. All I could think about was Paul being hurt. I can remember giving directions as though I were mistress of the house, helping to pull off Paul's raincoat, ordering Ora to help him upstairs. As for Ron, he existed only on the fringe of my consciousness as a sort of malevolent force. It did not occur to me to wonder whether or not he had been hurt as well. Leaving him still leaning against the door, I hurried upstairs after Ora and Paul.

I flung open the door to Paul's bedroom, then, while Ora helped him into a chair, I swept Eileen's clothes off the bed and pushed them under it. There would be time enough to explain what Miranda had done later. As for the skirt and sweater I was wearing, I could only hope that he would not notice. There had been enough tragedy in the past few hours for him to bear. I did not want to remind him of past tragedies as well.

Paul had leaned his head back against the chair, one hand still pressing his forehead in a vain attempt to stop the flow of blood. His skin was ashen. Leaving Ora to hover awkwardly over him, I hurried into the bathroom and came back with a wet washcloth which I used to wipe away the blood, pushing his hand gently away. The wound was not as deep as I had feared, but it stretched across half of his forehead. It would obviously require a good many stitches, and even then there would be a scar. Helplessly, I remembered that we could not even get a doctor here.

"See if there's some disinfectant in the cabinet in the bathroom," I told Ora. "And bring me some gauze and tape."

Paul's eyes were closed. "Is everything all right here?" he muttered. "Is Miranda——"

"She's asleep," I said. "I gave her something to make her sleep. It's all right. Enoch is with her. What happened, Paul? For God's sake, what happened?"

"We didn't see that the bridge was out until too late." His voice was so faint that I had to bend close to his lips to hear him. "There must have been some sort of tidal bore."

"And Devlon? The inspector?"

"Farrow claimed he dived for him." Paul rolled his head back and forth on the cushioned back of the chair. "He said he couldn't even find the car. There was a terrific current. I don't know how I made it to the bank. We've got to let someone know."

"That's the impossible part of it," Ora said bluntly, handing me a bottle of alcohol. "Until this storm stops we're as good as on an island, and that's a fact."

There was something comforting about the clumsy good nature of the man. He stood beside me, handing me what I needed as I bandaged the wound, and he talked as though there were no end to what he had to say. We heard a long recital of the characteristics of past storms he had known and how he had seen this one "making up," as he put it, all week. As I gently wiped the blood from Paul's matted hair, he told us about how he had heard the car speeding past his cottage and hurried out in an attempt to warn whoever it was that the bridge might not be safe.

"It's just over the rise beyond my place," he explained, his blunt face tight with the effort of trying to explain. "Now, there may have been a tidal bore, or there may not. I was thinking that if there had been, I would have heard it. As t'was, I didn't know the bridge was already down and the estuary flooding into the meadow. Should have kept a better watch, I should. Fact that I live so close by makes me responsible."

"No," Paul said wearily, "don't blame yourself. I've lived around here nearly as long as you have. I've seen these storms. I know what can happen. If I hadn't had so many other things on my mind—if there had been more light——"

"No one's to blame," I said. "You can't even be certain that the inspector didn't escape. You simply may not have seen him. He may have managed to get out on the other side of the estuary. You said the light wasn't good."

"It's good enough for me to tell you there's not much hope the man's alive," Ora assured me. He made as if to plunge his hands in his trouser pockets and looked down at himself in a puzzled way, as though he had just realized that he was still wearing his slicker. "I ran all the way, you see. Heard the brakes scream and everything. By the time I got there the car was nowhere in sight. Under water. Then I saw two men come to the surface. Mr. Randolph here and that other fellow downstairs. Farrow. No one else. It was raining hard and all, but I would have seen him if he'd come up. I kept my eyes——"

A crash sounded. Ora swore, and Paul jerked himself upright in the chair. "It's all right," I said, recognizing the sound. "Just some slate being blown off the roof. It happened before."

"Now, there's a thing that ought to be seen to," Ora said as though relieved there was now some problem with which he could actively concern himself. "I'll just go up in the attic and take a look. There's a trapdoor up there leads out to the roof."

"I can't let you do that," Paul said as Ora started toward the door. "It isn't safe."

"Now, I don't mean to go out on the roof, Mr. Randolph," Ora said. "I'm not as great a fool as that. But one look can tell me what's going on up there. I've known these roofs man and boy. . . ."

Still talking, he opened the door and left us. Paul smiled faintly. "His father was general caretaker here for years," he said, "and when he died, Ora took over. He'll feel better if he's doing something." His smile faded. "And, God knows, so would I. I suppose the phone is out."

"Yes," I said. Instead of dying, the storm seemed to be growing in violence. Beyond the drawn drapes the rain pounded on the windows. "I was just trying to get in touch with you when you came back," I added.

"In touch with me?" The color was coming back into his face now. His eyes met mine. The bandage across his forehead seemed to fracture his features, but his eyes were direct. For a moment what had happened meant nothing. We were simply two people who could merge into one. The tenderness on his face told me that he knew it, too. He cleared his throat and looked away. "Why should you have tried to get in touch?" he said. "I thought you said that everything was all right."

"It's all right only because Miranda is in bed and asleep," I said. "I had to give her two of the pills she generally takes at night. She—she thought it was night, and so there was no trouble."

"She was upset, then?" He enunciated each word carefully, as though there were some chance I might not understand him.

I shrugged. For some reason I did not want to talk

about Miranda now, perhaps because I wanted to give him some sort of respite from trouble, perhaps because—no, that was as far as I would go. There was no point now in examining my motives. And I had to tell him.

"Yes," I went on in a rush. "She was upset, as you put it. You saw the way she looked when she and the inspector came out of the den. I tried to go up to her, but——"

"I remember," Paul said impatiently. "Devlon didn't want you to talk to her."

"When I came up here to get my sweater, I found Enoch just coming out of your father's library."

"Did you?" Paul frowned. "What was he doing in there?"

"I don't know. I didn't ask him. I thought it was more important that he understand what had happened so that perhaps he could cope——"

"You told him that Miranda had reported to Devlon that I killed my father?"

"Yes. Perhaps I shouldn't have explained, but at the time it seemed to be the only thing to do. I hoped that he could talk her into some sort of reasonable state."

"You think that her—her testimony was unreasonable then?"

I nodded. "Yes. I can't accept the fact that you killed him."

For a moment neither of us spoke. The only sound was the howling of the wind outside. There was another crash as a tile struck the ground. I thought of Ora—but only for a moment.

Paul took a deep breath. "Well," he said, "I take it that Enoch wasn't able to do anything with her."

I put the roll of gauze on the table and sank down on the footstool at Paul's feet. "After you and the inspector left," I said carefully, "I went to the kitchen to tell Mrs. Herrick about the response she should make when your lawyer called to say that he'd arrived in Truro."

"Manson," Paul muttered. "My God, I'd forgotten him.

He's not going to like being stranded in Truro with no way of even getting in touch with me."

"That's his problem, isn't it?" I said, and now it was my turn to be impatient. I wanted to lead up to what I had to tell him about Miranda very carefully. If he began thinking of his solicitor, it would only make it more difficult for him to take in what had happened to his wife.

"Yes, that's his problem," Paul said wearily. "You were going to tell me. . . ."

"That while I was talking with Mrs. Herrick the first tile blew off the roof. I went outside to see what had happened, and——"

"It wasn't too clever, your doing that." For a moment Paul's hand tightened on my arm. "You could have been struck. One of those tiles could kill a person."

It was so obvious that he truly cared that I could have wept. I felt his hand on mine. "It was only for a moment," I said. "But when I came up here, I realized that I was soaking wet." I tried to laugh. "And, miraculously enough, there were clothes spread out on the bed." I watched him carefully. "Not mine," I added.

"I don't know what point you're trying to make," Paul said.

"You don't recognize this skirt and sweater?"

"No. They're not the sort of thing you wear, are they? No, I don't recognize them. It's a common tweed and——"

"They're Eileen's things," I said.

He stared at me without speaking.

"Miranda had kept them in a drawer in one of her bureaus," I said. "A drawer she could lock. Enoch was there with her when she tried to get them out. The key was broken, so he forced the drawer for her. It was directly after she'd seen the inspector. Apparently she didn't say a word to Enoch about what she'd told Devlon. She was the same as she was this morning when she came into this room and woke me. The only thing she could talk about was how much better life was going to be now—now that your father was dead."

Paul's dark eyes narrowed. "You didn't tell me that," he said.

"There wasn't any time," I reminded him. "The point is, she told Enoch that now that your father was dead, Eileen was coming back. That was why she had to get out her clothes."

"But you said you found the clothes spread out on this bed. Not in the room that used to be Eileen's down the hall. But here where she knew you were staying."

I had broken it to him as gradually as I dared, gone far enough in the telling so that he could make his own guesses.

"You?"

I scarcely heard the word. I nodded.

"She thinks that you're Eileen?"

"Yes. I didn't know what to do then, so—so I gave her the pills and pretended that it was night."

Suddenly I had an overwhelming need to see that she was still sleeping, that there was still some time to talk alone before we were interrupted, caught up in the urgencies of the moment. I hurried to the door and opened it quietly. She was still asleep and apparently had not moved from the position she had been in when I left her. Her dark hair still fanned the pillow. As for Enoch, he was asleep as well, his chin sunk heavily on his chest. I could hear the faint sound of his snores.

"I'm sorry," I told Paul, returning to the footstool, "but I had to be sure. It's all right. They're both asleep."

"Enoch, too." For a moment Paul smiled, and it was a fond smile. I realized suddenly that although I knew a good deal about the workings of this household now and the interrelations of people in it, I did not know how the older and younger man felt about one another. For all that I knew Paul might have been angry to hear that I had, as a matter of fact, turned Miranda over to Enoch's care.

"Well," he said, "we'll face the problem of how to deal with Miranda when we have to. Perhaps I should have insisted that she go into a hospital before now, but she didn't want to, and to commit her as long as she was sometimes rational—that and the fact that her doctors told me there was little more they could do for her in an institution than I could do. But I don't have to rationalize to you."

"No," I said, "you don't."

For a moment we sat in utter peace. Even the wind seemed to give some respite. It was very quiet. He could be, I realized with a flare of joy, at peace with me. He had had little enough peace in his life. His hand slipped to my wrist, and then our palms were pressed together, fingers outstretched and touching. It was as intimate as if our bodies, too, had touched. I knew that I should feel guilty, but I was conscious only of a great joy.

"It seems incredible that we should just be sitting here," Paul said finally. "I feel as though we should be doing something, making some attempt to get in contact with someone."

"What can we do?" I demanded. "You say there's no chance that the inspector is alive."

"I don't see how he could be. Either he would have surfaced as Ron and I did immediately or. . . ." He shrugged. "He may have had every intention of bringing a murder charge against me, but I wouldn't have wished this on him. Perhaps, though, you're right. I ought to go back down to the estuary."

"No," I protested. "Not with your head in that condition."

"I suppose," Paul said, "that back in Truro they'll assume Devlon is still here with me. It won't occur to anyone to come out looking for us. As far as I know, he hadn't made any definite plans to bring me back there with him. Not until he talked to Miranda. But I suppose when they do find out what happened, they may think that I was somehow responsible for his death. That isn't true, you know, Sara. When we went into the water, the door on my side was pulled open. There wasn't any question of my struggling to get out of the car, of trying to get anyone else out. The car plunged into the estuary, and I was pulled out into the water. Ron was sitting between Devlon and me. The same thing must have happened to him. The combination of the storm and the tides made it a—a caldron. There wasn't any possibility of our diving to see if we could get him out. It was all we could do to get to shore ourselves. I don't even know what happened to my forehead. I must have struck the windshield when we went off into the water. But when the police know that he was, in all probability, going to charge me with murder. . . ."

"They don't have to know," I said in a low voice. "After all, he took the step because of Miranda's statement, didn't he? By the time someone else talks to her, she may not say the same thing. And that's the only real basis for a charge, isn't it? Her statement that she saw you kill your father?"

"There's Ron," Paul said slowly.

"He has no way of knowing what Miranda told the inspector," I reminded him. "Unless you spoke of it in the car."

"No." Paul shook his head. "No one said anything in that car. I suppose you're right. But I'm the only person who seems to have had, to quote the inspector, access to the murder weapon—or the means—the opportunity, and a clear-cut motive."

"Motive!" I cried. "It's not your fault that you are your father's heir."

"Look, Sara," Paul said, bending forward in his chair until his face was very close to mine, "you've got to view this as the inspector saw it, as whoever takes over for him is bound to see it. To them I'm a man who gave up his career and the society of other people to come here and be tied here by a demanding old man who had to be waited on hand and foot and an unstable wife who has to be

watched constantly. That sort of thing is enough to drive a
good many men to murder."

"But you came here because you wanted to save Pennarth and because you loved your father and he needed
you."

"No," Paul said in a low voice, "I didn't love him, Sara.
He'd done a good many ugly things."

"Eileen?" I whispered.

"If you mean was he responsible for her death, yes, in a
way he was. They found out at the school that she was
pregnant. When she came back here, he made life unen-
durable for her. I don't know what happened the night she
died, but if she deliberately killed herself, it was in good
part because of him."

"All right," I said helplessly, "but the police don't know
how you felt about him. And simply being his heir——"

"Nothing is ever simple," Paul said slowly. His hand
slipped away from mine. He stared past me. "I've been his
heir since I was twenty-one. Logically, if that had been
enough to induce me to kill him, I could have done so
long before this. But there's more. For the last few months
my father wasn't content to let me handle the running of
the clay mines. I told you once that it is the source of our
capital. Do you remember?"

I thought of the way the sun had shone that day he
drove me back from St. Ives and the white mounds of clay
in the distance. I remembered how happy I had been to
find that we were not enemies and how much it had hurt
at the end of the drive to find that he mistrusted me. But
that no longer mattered.

"Yes," I said. "I remember."

"Lately my father had been in direct contact with the
manager of the mines," Paul said slowly. "Giving his own
orders. Countermanding mine. It was his last chance, I
suppose, to prove that he still had power. There was no
way I could stop him. But he was doing a lot of damage to
the business. He was out of touch. If he had lived another

six months, he would have ruined us. I think the inspector had talked to the mine manager. I think he knew all about that part of it. And that means he realized that only if my father died was there any hope of saving Pennarth."

The sound that shattered his voice was not that of slate falling from the roof. It was a loud, hollow, vibrating sound that lingered and faded and died and then began again.

"What is it?" I demanded, clutching Paul's arm.

"It sounds like the Chinese gong in the hall," he said, puzzled. He rose. "No one's rung that thing for years. My mother was rather fond of it. She associated it with her childhood when it was always used to call them to meals. She tried to convince my father that we should use it here, but—" Paul smiled dryly—"my father wasn't the sort of man who indulged women's fancies, as he called them."

The gong was rung again, the dull, expanding sound rising over the screaming of the wind about the corners of the house. "You don't suppose that it's Miranda?" I said.

In answer Paul went to the connecting door between the two bedrooms, as I had done a few minutes earlier, and opened it noiselessly. He shook his head, closed it again, then returned.

"No," he said. "Both of them are still asleep. But they won't be for long if whoever that is isn't made to stop striking that thing."

Both of us had forgotten Ron's presence in the house. I was shocked into remembrance when we came to the bottom of the stairs and saw him just about to level the padded hammer at the huge gold Chinese gong which he had pushed into the middle of the great hall. We stood on the landing caught in the rectangle of pale light pouring through the window behind us and watched the scene below us in silence.

Ron was not alone. I think Paul would have announced his presence if he had been. After all, we had come down to tell whoever it was that the noise must stop. But, it seemed, Mrs. Herrick had reached the hall before us. She stood in front of Ron, her hands on her hips. I could not see her face, but her shoulders were stiff with anger.

"Stop that noise!" she said in a shrill voice that cut its way up to us through the shadows.

Ron lowered the padded hammer and stared at her. It was difficult to see the expression on his face because we were standing above him and because the shadows of the hall were so deep, but I heard him laugh. It was a thick, guttural sound.

"You've been drinking," Mrs. Herrick said accusingly. "What are you doing back here, anyway? You're supposed to be in Truro with Mr. Randolph and the inspector."

I realized suddenly that no one had told her either of Paul's return or of the circumstances surrounding it. I started down the stairs, but Paul caught my hand and held me back. I obeyed him.

"Perhaps we decided to come back," Ron said, and the difference in his voice made me know that she was right, that he had been drinking. "You don't think," he went on, "I'm about to tell you anything that I don't want the whole of Cornwall to know about the next day, do you?"

"I don't know what you're talking about," the woman hissed, stretching her neck toward him. "You're like your father and your father's father before him. No good."

So they did know one another. I caught my breath. Paul's hand was still on my arm. He did not move.

"You don't know anything about me," Ron said thickly. There was only the distance of a few feet between them, but he moved toward her, raising the padded hammer with which he had struck the gong as he came. She faced him, rigid.

"I know enough about you," the housekeeper said. The great hall threw her voice upward.

"And what's that supposed to mean?"

"That you're up to no good. All you ever caused us is trouble."

"Caused you?" He lowered the hammer and laughed again. "I never had anything to do with you. You're the one that causes trouble. You're the one who spread it all over the village that Eileen was pregnant."

"And you're the one who made her that way." There was so much viciousness in the way she spoke that involuntarily I shrank back behind Paul.

"Bitch!" Suddenly Ron threw his head back and saw us. With his eyes still on us he struck the gong hard with a backhanded motion of the padded hammer. The hollow roar trembled on the air as he stared at us defiantly. The housekeeper followed his gaze, half turning.

"We'll have lunch now, Mrs. Herrick," Paul said calmly, dropping my hand and preceding me down the stairs.

If the housekeeper was disconcerted at seeing us, she did not show it. "For three?" she said sullenly.

"For three." Paul had reached the foot of the stairs. "If you don't mind not sounding that gong again, Farrow," he said in a hard voice, "I'd appreciate it. My wife is asleep, and I'd just as soon she stayed that way."

Ron looked back and forth between us, his eyes insolent. "I imagine that you would," he said.

Mrs. Herrick vanished through the green-baize door, slamming it behind her. Paul went up to Ron and took the hammer away from him and placed it beside the gong. "And another thing," he said, as though the younger man had not spoken, "I don't think there's much to be gained from talking about my sister now."

Ron went to a low marble-topped table near the hooded fireplace and picked up a glass half filled with wine. "I helped myself to what I could find in the cabinet in the dining room," he muttered. "I don't know about you, but I needed a drink."

Paul shrugged. "The only point I'm trying to make," he said, "is that since we have to stay here together until the storm lets up, we might as well try to behave in——"

"In a civilized manner? My God, I don't believe in you,

Randolph. I wouldn't have thought I could even imagine you."

Paul turned away from him and started toward the dining room. Through the open door I could see one of the maids hurriedly setting the table.

"Things have turned out pretty well for you anyway, haven't they, Randolph?" Ron said in a loud voice. "With the inspector dead you can begin to think of things getting back to normal, can't you?"

Paul was in the dining room now. I stood in the doorway and watched him take two wineglasses out of a cabinet at the side of the room. The maid, the same girl I had passed earlier in the upstairs corridor carrying linen, finished laying the silver and hurried out of the room by a small door set flush in the paneled wall.

"Will you have some sherry, Sara?" Paul said.

"Yes," I said in a low voice as Ron came to stand beside me.

He was obviously a bit unsteady on his feet, and I moved toward the table to avoid having him close to me. He was looking at me sharply, and it occurred to me that he might recognize the clothes I had on. Somehow the idea repelled me, and for a moment I thought of hurrying upstairs to change into my own skirt and blouse, whether they were dry or not. But I did not want to leave these two men together.

Paul was keeping himself in tight control, but I sensed what it must be costing him. Ron would not have to say much more to push him too far. The lights were on in this room, and I could see that the faces of both men were set and white. There was a nightmare quality in the atmosphere, as though something irrevocable was about to happen. And, for me, there was the agony of not being able to prevent it.

Paul handed me the wineglass. He did not look at Ron.

"You make a very attractive couple, as they say," Ron said, raising his own glass to his lips. "Cheers."

"Look here, Farrow," Paul murmured in a low voice. "In the past few minutes you've tried everything you can think of to make me angry. And I want to know why."

Ron started to speak, his mouth twisted scornfully, but at that moment Ora Johnson appeared behind him in the doorway, his slicker glistening with moisture. Water trickled down the creases of his weathered face. He seemed to be completely unaware that he was interrupting anything.

"I've been out on the roof," he said in his deep voice. "And a tricky bit of business it was, too. Now, there's something I can do to keep every tile on that roof from sliding off, but I don't want to do it without permission. If I could have a word with you, sir. . . ."

Paul nodded and led the way into the hall. The tension seemed to snap as he left the room. The maid appeared with a chafing dish, which she set on the buffet. I watched her hurry back toward the paneled door, casting Ron a curious glance as she went. Looking at him, I saw that his face was working. As I watched, his fingers tightened on the wineglass he was holding, snapping the stem.

"You've got to control yourself," I said in a low voice. Now that Paul was no longer in the room, I felt I must do something to right this situation. If it could ever be righted.

With what seemed to be an effort Ron's eyes focused on me. "Why in God's name are you wearing her clothes?" he muttered.

A core of ice seemed to solidify inside me. In a way I felt as though I should explain, but I did not want to talk about Miranda now. Something told me it would do nothing but worsen matters if Ron knew that she had taken it into her head to mistake me for Eileen, that she should have brought out Eileen's clothes for me.

"That doesn't matter," I said. "Sit down. Here. I'll pick up the glass. Don't drink any more, Ron. Promise me that. It will only make things more difficult."

I surprised myself with the reasonableness of my own voice. I had every reason to mistrust this man. Anyone who had acted as erratically as he should be mistrusted. First he had presented himself as a young artist who could talk about an old love affair with simple regret. I remembered how attractive I had found him when he had lain supine in the grass of Bertha's garden. There was nothing about him now that seemed the same. His face was sallow under its tan, and his eyes were red-rimmed.

No, I did not really know him, and there was little about him for me to sympathize with, since he so obviously hated Paul. The night he had come to see me at the cottage I had sensed that under the surface he was very close to losing control. Since then he had lost it. There had been no reason for him to go to the inspector and, if what he said was true, attempt to defend himself against lies someone—perhaps myself—was supposed to have told. There was no reason for him to have behaved with so much antagonism toward Paul. And yet, against all odds, I felt the absolute necessity of convincing him to be reasonable, even if I had to pretend to something I did not know in order to make him feel as vulnerable as he wanted Paul to feel.

"Don't try to interfere," he muttered, sinking down on one of the chairs that lined the table.

"What's wrong with you?" I said sharply. "Do you think that unless Paul is arrested, there may be some reason for the police to suspect you?"

He glanced at me, then leaned his chin in his hand and sat staring at the long rain-spattered windows. The lights flickered and died, and I felt a flood of anxiety as I realized that our last contact with the world was broken. It was as dusky in the room now as if it were evening. Ron did not appear to notice.

"No one's going to suspect me of anything," he muttered.

"Then why did you go to the inspector this morning?" I demanded. "It's just as logical that the police suspect you as that they suspect Paul. You could have gotten into this house. You were on the grounds at the time Mr. Randolph was murdered."

"But I didn't have a motive, did I?" His eyes flickered toward me and then away again.

"I think," I said, "that a clever lawyer could make it appear quite conceivable that you might have been in a state of mind last night to have committed murder. As far as how clear-cut the motive might have been, I imagine that a good many murderers have less reason to do what they do than any number of other people who know the victim."

"You don't know what you're talking about," Ron told me in a muffled voice.

"All right," I said, "think of this. You admitted to me that you had been able to keep the thought of Eileen's death pushed fairly far back in your mind for ten years. Then you met me at Bertha and Greg's, and you found out that I was living at the cottage where you used to meet her, and it all came back to you—all the things you thought you had managed to forget. By the time you came to see me last night you were in what a psychiatrist might describe as a 'disturbed' condition. You can't deny that."

"I'm not denying anything," Ron said in a low voice, staring at the table, "except that I didn't kill anyone."

"It doesn't matter what you did or didn't do," I reminded him. "What matters is what the police believe you might have done. Are you convinced, for example, that Inspector Devlon was certain Paul was guilty? If that was so, why did he really bring you out here? Why was he taking you back to Truro with Paul? Because he was going to do that, wasn't he? He wasn't going to make a side trip to St. Ives to drop you off."

I was playing this strictly by ear, but I sensed that the only way to defend Paul was to attack Ron. It was the only thing I could do now. Perhaps later there would be more, and whatever needed to be done, I would do it. The very realization of my commitment comforted me.

"You still haven't told me what motive I could possibly have had," Ron muttered. "You're just talking to hear yourself talk. Well, go on, if it makes you feel any better."

The maid came back into the dining room, carrying another dish, which she set on the sideboard. I glanced out into the hall and saw that Paul was still talking to Ora. I saw him move his arms as though he were arguing with him. The maid hurried out of the room.

"All right," I said. "So perhaps it does make me feel better. I think a case could be made for you having suddenly faced the fact of Eileen's death after ten years and— and not being able to cope with it. You know that her father must have made her life a misery after he found out that she was expecting a child. You were the only person who could have saved her, but you didn't. And so, subconsciously, you must have blamed him. People never blame themselves."

"Why should I blame myself?" he cried, staggering to his feet. "I suppose Miranda has been talking to you. Well, you ought to know by now that you can't believe anything that madwoman says."

So there was something Miranda might have told me that would have cast some degree of guilt on him. Not on Paul, but on him. I decided to play for time.

"You're contending that nothing Miranda might say could be accepted in a court of law?" I asked him.

"I didn't say that." He lurched toward me, grasping my arms. "What did she tell you about me?"

"What makes you think she could have told me anything?"

"I'm not an absolute fool," Ron muttered. "You got those clothes from her. No one else in this house would have kept them all these years. And if Miranda kept Eileen's clothes, she must have kept her diary. Well, I'm telling you that you can't believe anything she says."

He was not being clear. I had never heard of a diary before, but it was reasonable to assume Eileen might have kept one and that if she had, Miranda would have saved it. But I did not know whether he meant that I couldn't believe anything that was in the diary or that Miranda would not tell the truth about anything she had read in it. At all events I had stumbled onto something. If I bluffed, he might tell me something I wanted to know.

"Perhaps I've seen the diary myself," I said.

"All right." He seemed to collapse as though his legs would no longer support him. Sinking back onto the chair, he covered his face with his hands. "All right," he said, "so you know about the letter. You know that Eileen was expecting me to meet her at the cottage that night. That's what you're getting at, isn't it? Do you suppose I've ever stopped hating myself for not being there to meet her? That's what's been driving me mad. If I had been there, she might not have killed herself. Don't you see, I couldn't have killed the old man. Not when I was as much at fault as he was. I killed Eileen just as surely as though I had pushed her off that cliff."

There was no chance for him to say more. Paul came back into the dining room with Ora bulking behind him.

"Here," Paul said, handing the workman a plate from the table. "We might as well eat before we leave. Help yourself to whatever's on the buffet." He turned to me. He was being deliberately brisk, and I guessed what he was going to say.

"Ora and I are going down to the estuary," he said. "No matter how doubtful it is that Devlon managed to survive, we can't just stay about here doing nothing. There's a chance he might have been able to get to shore."

"No chance," Ora muttered. "I saw it happen, didn't I? We'd be better off trying to do something about them slates."

"The tide is starting to go out now," Paul went on as though Ora had not spoken. "It's possible that even with

the flooding we may be able to ford the estuary and get in
contact with the police at Truro."

Ron remained slumped in his chair as though he did not
hear. Obviously he meant to do nothing to stop them.

"You can't go," I said in a low voice. "Your head. . . ."

"I'm all right now," Paul told me. "You must see that I
can't just stay here and wait."

I went to the window and looked out. There was mist
now, as well as rain, wind-swirled mist that wove grotesque patterns about the swaying trees. I pressed my forehead against the glass and felt Paul's hands on my shoulders.

"If you're afraid to be here alone," he said softly, "I'll
stay, Sara."

I knew in that moment that no matter what our relationship was or had been or would be, I could never be a
burden to him. His life had been too full of burdens already. If he felt that he must search for the inspector, no
matter what the odds of finding him alive, then I must not
keep him here.

"I won't be alone," I murmured. "I'll relieve Enoch.
He'll want to have lunch. I can sit with Miranda until you
come back."

His hands tightened on my shoulders, and he pulled me
slowly around until I faced him. Beyond us Ora was standing at the buffet wolfing some food from his plate, an
incongruous figure in the narrow elegant room. Ron still
sat at the table, his head buried in his hands.

"Listen to me, Sara," Paul said in a voice so low that I
knew they could not hear. "Promise me one thing. Don't
stay alone with Miranda. Before I go I'll tell Mrs. Herrick
to go up to her."

"But why?" I whispered, bewildered. "That's why I'm
here. To help her."

"I don't think you can help her any longer," Paul said
slowly. "Not now when she believes that you're Eileen."

"I can play the role," I protested. "What does it matter

as long as it satisfies her? As soon as we can get a doctor, it will be different, but now it's the only thing to do. Besides, when she wakes up, she may have—come to her senses. I mean, she may see everything the way it really is then."

"No!" Paul no longer bothered to lower his voice. "I can't take the risk. You mean too much to me. Don't you see, Sara. . . ."

I did not dare to let him go on. There were things to be said between us. No matter what happened, they would be said, but not now, not here.

"There's no danger," I told him.

"We can't be certain." His eyes held mine as tightly as his hands. "We can't forget that last night someone was murdered in this house."

"But you don't think that she—"

He shook his head. His face was very pale. "I don't know what to think," he said. "When the inspector insisted that I go with him, I had no option. I wasn't thinking clearly. Too much had happened in such a short space of time. As soon as we drove away from the house, I realized that we might be leaving the murderer behind. Because I didn't do it, Sara. I'm the only one who knows that, but I do know it. And now. . . ."

He moved away from me abruptly, jamming his hands in the pockets of his slacks as though he no longer dared to maintain the physical contact between us.

"And now," he said, "I feel a moral responsibility to look for Devlon. I never would have left the scene of the accident in the first place if I hadn't been dazed. And yet, perhaps you're right. Perhaps I shouldn't leave you. . . ."

"I told you I would be all right," I reminded him, keeping my voice calm. I guessed that this was one of the rare times in his life when he had not been able to make a decision. And I understood. If, by any chance, the inspector had managed to escape from the car alive, if he had managed to get to the shore and was lying there hurt, then Paul would never forgive himself if he did not go.

"Ora can go alone," he said abruptly.

The hulking man standing draped in his slicker by the buffet raised his head. "It's a fool's errand," he muttered.

Paul glanced at him and then back to me. "You see," he said, "he's so convinced that Devlon's dead that he'll never make a real search. I know the man. The only thing he lacks is an imagination. But in this case imagination is important. I have to go. Will you promise me that you'll let Mrs. Herrick stay with Miranda? If you gave her two of those pills, she may not wake up for some time yet at any rate."

I agreed. There was nothing else I could do. I watched as he dug a raincoat very much like Ora's from the hall closet. "I'll ask Mrs. Herrick to go upstairs," I said as he started toward the green-baize door.

Paul held open the door and ushered a still-grumbling Ora through it. In a moment they were gone, snatched away from me by the raging storm. I had forgotten Ron, and my heart caught in my throat as he lurched past me through the shadows of the hall.

"Where are you going?" I demanded with an assurance I did not feel.

For a moment he turned to face me, swaying slightly, but his voice, when he spoke, was no longer thick. "Does it matter?" he said.

The drunken man became boy again, just as in Bertha's garden I had seen the boy behind the man. I was not certain of anything about him now except his misery. And I could do nothing about that. Even to tell him that it mattered to me if he left would be a lie. It would be a relief to have him gone. We both knew that. But in the face of his anguish I had to speak.

"You won't be any help to Paul and Ora now," I said softly. "Wait a bit."

Slowly he came toward me. In the dusk of the great hall

I could not see his face. "You don't want to stay here with a murderer," he muttered, pausing an arm's length from me.

I could not speak. I tried and heard the strangled sound that should have been words.

"Don't worry," Ron said. "I've done enough. . . ."

The roar of the wind down the chimney blotted out whatever else he said. I watched, motionless, as he wrenched open the huge oak door and disappeared. I saw his raincoat lying in a crumpled heap near the Chinese gong. He had gone out into the storm without protection of any sort—he meant to kill himself.

It was an absurd idea. I stood watching the rain lashing at the long windows through the half light and sternly told myself that I was letting my imagination run away with me.

When he said that I would want him to go because I would not want to be alone with a murderer, he was just being sarcastic. Yet, I had heard him suggest that he could have killed Paul's father. I had never really believed that. Or had I?

If he had meant anything, it was that he was responsible for Eileen's death. The idea had lain in wait at the back of his mind for too long and had grown roots that threatened to strangle his reason. He had done an ugly thing by not going to Eileen when she had needed him. But all of us hurt those we love or have loved in the moment when they seem to be asking us to pay too great a price. He had been only a boy.

We were all guilty in a sense for what had happened to Eileen and all the frightened girls like her. There was so much that was ugly in life. When I lied to him about having seen the diary, a diary I was not even certain existed, I, too, was guilty of a cruel deception.

A sensation of dread settled over me. The old house echoed with the sounds of the wind. In the minstrel's gallery a board creaked. I did not fear for my own safety.

Instead I was afraid for the others, for Miranda sunk in the pit of her own madness, for Paul who might risk his own safety in his attempt to find the inspector, for Ron wandering in a state of confusion through the storm.

I thought of the night I had run through the mist and nearly fallen headlong into the sea. But surely, even in the condition that he was in, Ron knew the grounds of this estate too well to be in the same sort of danger. Unless he deliberately—but I could not let myself think of that possibility, because there was nothing I could do. For the first time I realized how trapped Paul must have felt here in the house. We were all trapped, and all that I could do was what he had asked me. Enoch was to be relieved by Mrs. Herrick, and then . . . there was nothing to do but wait.

I found the housekeeper in the kitchen. Candles had been lit on the long sideboard, and in their flickering glow the two maids bent close together over the sink. Taking one of the candles, I asked Mrs. Herrick to come up to Miranda's room as soon as she could. My voice was expressionless with weariness. She inclined her head. The two girls whispered together, throwing frightened glances over their shoulders as though I represented some malignant force. I left them and slowly climbed the back stairs to the second story, the candle throwing fingers of light in front of me.

Without thinking I tried Miranda's door, realizing only as I turned the knob that it was locked. Going on to my room—Paul's room—I made my way to the adjoining door between the bedrooms. It was still ajar. Miranda was still stretched motionless on the bed, with Enoch asleep in the chair beside it. The candlelight softened his old features as I went to him and touched his arm.

He came awake quite suddenly, as old people do, moving effortlessly from one dream to another. He smiled at me, and I felt the warmth of the reassurance that being with him always brought me. Slowly he pushed himself out of the chair and shuffled after me into Paul's bedroom.

"I must apologize, my dear," he puffed as I partially closed the door to shut out the sound of our voices. "I was supposed to be watching, and I slept."

"She's still asleep," I said. "It doesn't matter. Mrs. Herrick is coming to sit with her soon. You'll want your lunch."

"Lunch?" He ran one gnarled hand over his face. "The light deceived me. I thought that it was night already."

A crash sounded—a single sharp definitive sound in a world filled with the roar of the storm.

"The lights are out," I said. I sank down on the side of the bed. Enoch took the candlestick from me. The flame flickered and almost died as he conveyed it shakily to the bedside table.

"My poor child," he said, puffing a bit as he lowered himself onto the bed beside me, "you look as though you were carrying the weight of the world on your shoulders."

I told him then about what had happened during the past few hours.

"I feel like Rip Van Winkle," he said when I had finished. "I sleep, and the world changes completely. No, not the world. Only the situation. It was a dreadful thing for the inspector to have been so arbitrary about Paul, but I am sure that we would have far rather that Paul had been charged than that innocent man should have been drowned." He puckered his face. "But," he said heavily, "if there is anything that a long life has taught me, it is that the Fates will make their own demands and it is useless to resist."

He was so short and bent that sitting on the edge of the bed, his legs did not reach the floor. He clenched his gnarled hands in his lap, and I was reminded of a schoolboy who had been rebuked. "Lena often said that I submitted too readily," he said as though talking to himself. "She told me to resist, but I was never strong enough until it was too late. Now that she is dead I have the papers. The police will find the drawer of his desk where the key was kept wrenched open, and they will ask questions. Oh, yes, because even with the inspector dead, they will come again. And I will tell them that it was me who opened the safe. The papers are burned. But if they insist, I will tell them what they contained."

"They would not punish an old man like myself for an error committed in my youth. Or if they did, it would not matter. But I should never have waited, you see. I should have risked everything while she was still alive. While I slept, I dreamed of her, and even in my dream she told me that I had been a coward."

He brushed one hand across his eyes, bending so low that I could not see his face under its thick mat of white hair. I did not know what he was talking about, but I sat very still, knowing that if he wanted to tell me, he would.

"And I am a coward still," I heard him mutter. His hand moved away from his eyes and sought mine. "Oh, yes, my dear," he murmured. "I can admit it to you. I let them take Paul away without confessing that I had as good a reason as he and better to have wanted his father dead."

Hunching himself about on the bed, he faced me. The old eyes that had always been so guileless faltered in the candlelight. "You see, my child," he went on, "when I was a mere youth in London, there was an—an unfortunate incident." He laughed hoarsely. "Ah, what a coward I am. Even now I cannot call it by its proper name."

"Call it what it was," I said in a low voice. It was clear to me now that he wanted desperately to tell me something. He was very old. Probably he was rambling. But if he wanted to confess a past peccadillo, he must do it. Even if this was not the time.

"Then I must call it murder," he whispered. "At the very least, manslaughter."

My first impulse was to repeat the words. But I resisted. I said nothing. To speak would be to show that I was horrified or confused or repelled or disbelieving.

"It was an accident," Enoch went on. "Not meant by me to happen. A drunken quarrel. We were both young, and he was a stranger. Can you believe that I have forgotten the details? Except one. I did not give myself up to the police. I went into service. The Randolph service. Because it would bring me here, far away from London."

He made a squeaking sound which I thought must be a sigh. "The master was a young man then. Not the sort to bother with references if someone suited him. And I suited him. But he guessed there was something in my past. He must have guessed, but he did nothing until Lena and I. . . . It was understandable that he would be upset. She was his sister. I was his valet.

"He could not allow anything to come of it. So he had my past investigated and obtained the proof he needed to control me. When Lena wanted me to go away with her, what could I do but refuse? She stayed here until her mother died. She was a woman grown. She told me that we were our own masters, and she could not understand why I could never leave Pennarth."

His head slumped on his chest. Gusts of wind forcing themselves around the windows made the candle glow shudder. "Did you tell her the truth?" I whispered.

"Cowards do not tell truths," the old man muttered. "She guessed that something was wrong, that somehow her brother was responsible. But she did not truly understand. She pretended to believe that I would not come to her because of some misbegotten idea of class. Now and then she would come to the cottage, and I would meet her there. And then for so many years there were only letters."

I did not know how to comfort him. "It's all in the past," I whispered.

"The past is the only thing I have."

It was said so simply that I wanted to weep. The wind bruised itself against the house, and the rain rattled the windows. "There was nothing you could do," I told him.

"I could have killed him long before."

"You did not kill him."

"How can you know that?" He straightened his back with an effort. "The point is, my dear, I must no longer procrastinate. I must tell the police that I had as great a reason as Paul to want him dead. Then they must prove or disprove, as they can. I am an old man. I cannot change my character completely. But I can give Paul a chance. I can tell them—"

A crash severed the words. For a moment I thought that it was more slate falling to the ground. And then I heard a woman scream.

I rushed into the next room. The housekeeper was on her knees groping for a candle that had apparently fallen onto the carpet from the candlestick she was holding. As I ran toward her, the flame caught the thick shag of the rug. I stamped it out and helped her to her feet. It was so dark that I could not see her face, but I could feel her shaking.

"She pushed me," I heard her gasp. "When I unlocked the door, she pushed me."

Enoch was standing in the doorway that connected the two bedrooms. He was holding the candle. In its shivering light I could see that the bed was empty.

"She's gone," Mrs. Herrick said, her voice rising shrilly. "There was nothing I could do to stop her. She said that unless she could find her, Eileen would die."

As Mrs. Herrick uttered Eileen's name, I heard the slamming of a heavy door below and remembered that when Ron had left, I had made no attempt to secure it, although I had known how anxious Paul was that Miranda not leave the house. A wave of guilt swept over me. He had left her in my care, and I had failed him.

"I'm going after her," I said, starting toward the open door.

"Don't be a fool!" For the first time Mrs. Herrick spoke to me as though I were an equal. Her bony hand gripped my arm and held me fast. "Let her go!" she hissed.

I heard Enoch groan and saw that he was bending laboriously to retrieve something from the floor. In the light of the shaking candle in his other hand I saw a white-paged book lying open on the carpet. Afraid that the effort the old man was making would topple him, I wrenched myself away from the housekeeper and went to pick it up for him. One glance was sufficient even in the flickering light to tell me that it was a diary. Thinly formed words tumbled down the white page as though the writer had not been able to control her hand. For it was a woman's hand. Eileen's. This was the diary Ron had mentioned.

My mind raced. If I were to leave the house without knowing where Miranda had gone, I would never find her. The estate was too vast, the rain and fog an impenetrable veil. My eyes darted around the room. There was no sign that she had dressed. Her nightgown was not on the bed. But the bottom drawer of the white bureau was open. It gaped emptily at me.

"Was that where she kept Eileen's clothes?" I demanded of Enoch.

He nodded, but there was no need for his affirmation as my eyes went back to the bureau and I saw the glitter of a gold key on top of it. The broken key. Symbolic of so much else that had been broken in this house. So many human desires shattered.

I took the candle from Enoch and held it steady over the open pages of the diary. The left-hand page was crammed full of that tortured writing. The right-hand page was empty. I shuffled the pages that followed. All empty. This, then, had been Eileen's last entry. Holding the candle close, I scanned the words.

In a few minutes I'm going to meet him at the cottage. I wrote him yesterday. He would have had the letter this morning. I didn't tell him why they brought me home. But in an hour he'll know. There's a heavy mist, but that won't stop him from meeting me.

And when I tell him, he'll take care of me. Oh, dear God, let him take care of me.

That was all. So few words. Written so long ago. And yet my eyes were stinging as I closed the book and handed it to Enoch. What must she have felt as she waited in the mist, as slowly she realized that Ron was not coming? His desertion that drove her to the cliff and to her death.

For a moment I hated not only Ron, but all men whose courage had failed them. Yet they suffered, too. I remembered the tormented look in Ron's eyes, the way Enoch had seemed to shrink inside his old body. In the end, perhaps, women had their own revenge, even if they found it in separation and death.

But I could not think of that now. The only thing that mattered was that Miranda had wakened still lost in her own confusion, that she had taken the diary from the drawer and managed to make out the words I had just read. She must have read them before. But now with her sense of time and person suspended, she must have thought that the Eileen she had seen personified in me was once again going to her death, and hoping to save her, she would have headed in the direction of the cottage. Now, at least, there was some hope that I might find her.

This time Mrs. Herrick did not try to stop me as I went out the door. As I ran down the curving stairs, I heard Enoch's voice raised in what might have been a protest. Wrenching open the heavy door, I ran out into the storm.

The wind swept me up in its arms, caressing my face with misty fingers. The storm was blowing from the north, and despite the muffling fog, I could hear the pounding of the surf. I had to steady myself against the trees as I ran down the gravel drive. My mind raged, like the storm, with its own confusion.

How would I deal with Miranda when I found her? If I found her. She knew the estate far better than I. In her haste to find Eileen she had doubtlessly taken the shortcut. The thought of making the same mistake I had made before, of passing the cottage and going straight toward the cliffs terrified me. But the mist was not as thick now, although the rain blinded me.

This time I would be careful. Once I had turned off into the trees, I would watch for the cottage on my right. There could be no mistakes. It would be safer to go all the way down the twisting drive to the gate and then make my way past the gatehouse to the cottage, but I dared not take the time. If Miranda found no one at the cottage—and of course she would not, since she was seeking a girl who was ten years dead—then she might go directly to the cliffs, and finding no one there, she would assume that Eileen had hurled herself onto the rocks. And might she not then follow suit? How could I know what she might do?

My clothes were soaked, the cashmere sweater clinging to my skin, the tweed skirt heavy against my legs. I wiped the rain from my face with my hand. My only guide to the path I had followed the afternoon before would be the stone boundary marker. I must not miss it. The wind pummeled me, and the crashing of the surf battered my ears.

How could the sea sound so close? I had never feared anything as I feared that sound now. And yet it was not the only danger. A murderer was about. Perhaps back at the house. At Pennarth. How could I know if Enoch had been trying to tell me that he had, in fact, killed the old man who had been his blackmailer? Or Mrs. Herrick. What did I know of her? Might she not have deliberately let Miranda go? And Ron?

But these were insane thoughts. Even if one of them was guilty, they could not have known that Miranda would escape the house. But were either of them to come upon her. . . . She had accused Paul of murder. She was a threat to him. Oh, God! Was it only rain, or were those tears that drenched my face? There was no use thinking these thoughts. The wind threw me to the side, and as I strove to keep my balance, I saw the stone marker.

My heart pounding in my throat, I turned off into the

trees. The rain was less penetrating here, and I realized
with relief that I could see the path. Thorns pricked my
skirt as I ran, tugging at me like skeletal hands. I kept my
eyes trained to the right, and then suddenly through the
swaying mass of trees and bushes, I saw a roof: the cottage!

I lost the path in my haste to get to it. Scarcely noticing
the wet leaves through which I pushed, the roots over
which I stumbled, I made my way to the low-eaved house.
I leaned, breathless, against the gate, staring at it as
though I had never seen it before. The front door was
closed, the windows dark with the drapes still pulled across
them as I had left them the afternoon before. I realized
with a pang that there was no refuge from the world inside
those stone walls now. I could not escape my own commitment. Miranda was not here. And that meant. . . . Oh,
God, if I could only be certain what that did mean!

And then I heard her voice, thin on the wind. "Eileen!"

She was on her way to the cliff. I ran along the hedge
and up the rise to the side of the cottage, calling her
name.

"Eileen!"

"I'm here! I'm here!"

Suddenly I saw her standing above me, only a few feet
away from the edge of the rocks. She turned, and I saw
the white oval of her face, the mouth open. The crashing
of the surf blotted out whatever she said. And then we
were standing close together, and my hand was on her
bare wet arm. Her skin was as cold as death. She pulled
me against her, the drenched silk of her nightgown pressed
against my face. The strands of her hair were like seaweed
about me.

"It's all right!" she cried. "He's dead. He can't persecute
you anymore. He's dead, Eileen! I killed him for you!"

In that moment the wind seemed to die. Below us the
sea ebbed with a great sucking sound. Even my heart
seemed to stop beating. And in the moment of silence I

heard the sound of men's voices behind us in the direction of the cottage. Terror struck me. No one must startle Miranda now. The edge of the cliff was too close. If she were startled, she might step back and. . . .

"Come with me," I said, pulling myself away from her. "Come back to the cottage."

Her arms tightened about me. "I want to tell you now!" she cried exultantly.

"No!" I tried to pull her with me. "Come with me!"

There was no sound behind us now—no voices, no footsteps on the rocks. The elements rushed against us again. The ocean crashed. The wind screamed. I tried again to pull her after me, and as I did, she caught my face in one hand. Her fingers bit into my flesh. She tilted my face up and stared down at me through a veil of rain.

"Who are you?" she cried. "You're not Eileen! Who are you?"

Her eyes were wild. Her hand went from my face to my shoulder. She shook me back and forth as though I were a doll. "Tell me where Eileen is?" she demanded. "Tell me!"

Her voice was like a seagull's cry. And all the time she spoke she pulled me upward toward the edge of the cliff. I reached up with both hands and tried to wrench myself away from her, but her fingers were like iron nails driven into my body. I tried to throw my entire weight away from her and, in so doing, sank to the rocks. But still she maintained her grasp. Nothing had changed except that now it was more difficult for her to draw me after her. My terror nearly blotted out the pain of the sharp stone against my knees.

The edge of the cliff could not be far behind her now. In a moment, in seconds, both of us would tumble over the edge unless I could somehow stop her. Her fingers were as dead and as strong as ice under my clawing hands. Useless, utterly useless, to try to detach myself from her. I could only attempt to throw her off balance, and even then her iron grip might not be released, but I must risk it. There was nothing for me to hold onto, and her strength was the strength of madness.

Lunging the upper part of my body toward her, I threw my arms about her knees. Her legs buckled under her, and she fell backward, her arms outspread. Her scream blended with mine. I tried to catch her, but she was gone, and the second scream was only my own. And then there came the roar of the surf and Paul's voice calling my name and then Miranda's. I answered him, but she did not. It was only then that my mind grasped the fact that she was gone.

I took a few staggering steps down the rocky slope, and suddenly his arms were about me. Again, like the pause between the beating of a pulse, the sound of the storm seemed to suspend itself. I raised my face to his.

"There was nothing you could do to save her, Sara," he said. "She might have taken you with her. Thank God—thank God, you're safe."

"Did you see it all?" The words seemed to burn my throat.

He nodded. Over his shoulder I saw Ron move out of the mist and toward the cliff edge. Involuntarily I gave a cry. My nerves seemed to shatter.

"It's all right," Paul said. "Leave him alone. He has his own thoughts. We all have our own thoughts. We could have tried to save her, but we were afraid that if she saw us, she might be startled and. . . ." He released me. I saw his shoulders slump as though the mist were heavy on him.

"Perhaps," he said, "we were wrong to stand by. Devlon gone. Miranda. . . ."

"She killed your father," I told him. It had to be said. If I waited, I knew it might be an impossible thing for me to say. Later, guilt might settle over us like the fog.

"I know." I could barely hear the words over the sighing of the wind—the dying wind. The storm was ending. I took his hand.

"Would you have sacrificed yourself to protect her?" I asked him.

"Perhaps. If it hadn't been for you, Sara, it wouldn't have mattered what happened to me. You know that, don't you?"

There was no need for me to answer. Together we started slowly down the hill. I glanced back only once and saw the dark shadow that was Ron standing motionless above the void. I knew that he was thinking not of the woman who, moments before, had fallen to her death, but of another time. There were, I knew, too many memories for any one of us to look now, in this moment, to the future. But the cottage lay below us, and beyond that, Pennarth. And beyond that, a world in which there could be happiness for all of us.

Other SIGNET Gothics You Will Enjoy

More SIGNET Gothics You'll Enjoy

☐ **WITCH'S HAMMER by Caroline Farr.** A young woman reporter interviewing a fabulous screen lover at his eerie castle delves into his strange past and uncovers a mysterious death. (#T5771—75¢)

☐ **HOUSE OF TOMBS by Caroline Farr.** A young woman studying archaeology on a remote island off the coast of Maine finds her life in peril when she uncovers a bizarre secret. (#T5770—75¢)

☐ **KILMENY IN THE DARK WOOD by Florence Stevenson.** Could Kilmeny escape the diabolic spell that encompassed her and the man she loved . . . ? (#T5711—75¢)

☐ **HOUSE OF DARK ILLUSIONS by Caroline Farr.** A nightmare lingered in the shadows of the great stone house. Would it engulf Megan and her newfound love . . . ? (#T5579—75¢)

☐ **THE TOWERS OF FEAR by Caroline Farr.** Ali Cavanagh came to Storm Towers expecting a pleasant vacation, but she soon found herself immersed in a terrifying web of mystery; a web that tightened around her, threatening her life . . . (#T5138—75¢)

☐ **BIANCA by Florence Stevenson and Patricia Hagan Murray.** Could an old house destroy a beautiful marriage? What was the forgotten tragedy which brought sorrow to all who dwelt within the aged mansion? (#T5434—75¢)

Have You Read these Bestsellers from SIGNET?

More SIGNET Bestsellers You Will Enjoy

☐ **THE FRENCH LIEUTENANT'S WOMAN by John Fowles.** By the author of The Collector and The Magus, a haunting love story of the Victorian era. Over one year on the N. Y. Times Bestseller List and an international bestseller. "Filled with enchanting mysteries, charged with erotic possibilities . . ."—Christopher Lehmann-Haupt, N. Y. Times   (#W4479—$1.50)

☐ **SONS by Evan Hunter.** By the bestselling author of T* Blackboard Jungle, this is a powerful novel about thre* generations of Tyler men, portraying grandfather* father, and son; their changing world and values.
                                                         (#Y4288—$1.25)

☐ **THE PRETENDERS by Gwen Davis.** The exciting bestseller about the jet-setters is a masterful portrait of their loves, lives and fears.   (#W5460—$1.50)

☐ **JENNIE, VOLUME I: The Life of Lady Randolph Churchill by Ralph G. Martin.** In JENNIE, Ralph G. Martin creates a vivid picture of an exciting woman, Lady Randolph Churchill, who was the mother of perhaps the greatest statesman of this century, Winston Churchill, and in her own right, one of the most colorful and fascinating women of the Victorian era.   (#E5229—$1.75)

☐ **JENNIE, VOLUME II: The Life of Lady Randolph Churchill, the Dramatic Years 1895–1921 by Ralph G. Martin.** The climactic years of scandalous passion and immortal greatness of the American beauty who raised a son to shape history, Winston Churchill. "An extraordinary lady . . . if you couldn't put down JENNIE ONE, you'll find JENNIE TWO just as compulsive reading!"— Washington Post   (#E5196—$1.75)

THE NEW AMERICAN LIBRARY, INC.,
P.O. Box 999, Bergenfield, New Jersey 07621

Please send me the SIGNET BOOKS I have checked above. I am enclosing $_____(check or money order—no currency or C.O.D.'s). Please include the list price plus 25¢ a copy to cover handling and mailing costs. (Prices and numbers are subject to change without notice.)

Name_____

Address_____

City_____State_____Zip Code_____
            Allow at least 3 weeks for delivery

EVOKE

THE

WISDOM

OF

THE

TAROT

THE SUN.

With your own set of 78, full-color cards—the Albano-Waite deck you have studied in THE TAROT REVEALED.
